Incentives Rule the World

A practical framework for redesigning incentives so individuals, organizations, and societies consistently act in ways that create long-term value rather than short-term harm.

By Laura Lee

Lauxon Publishing, LLC

Published by Lauxon Publishing, LLC

For permission requests, please contact:
Email: info@Lauxonpublishing.com
Website: www.Lauxonpublishing.com

AUTHOR NOTE

This book was written to illuminate a simple truth: human behavior is predictable when we understand the incentives that guide it. Every choice, policy, and system is shaped by the rewards and penalties embedded within it, whether we notice them or not. My goal is not merely to explain these dynamics, but to give you the tools to shape them intentionally—so that your work, your communities, and your life align with values that truly matter. I believe that understanding incentives is a pathway to both ethical leadership and personal empowerment. This book is an invitation to notice the invisible forces that drive our decisions and to harness them to create meaningful, lasting change.

Table of Contents

Part IV — Incentives in Government, Policy, and Power

Part V — Incentives in Culture, Media, and Technology

Part VI — Designing Better Incentive Systems

Part VII — Incentives for a Sustainable Future

Prologue

We live in a world where intentions rarely equal outcomes. We watch policies fail, organizations stumble, and individuals act in ways that seem contrary to their values—and yet the patterns are rarely mysterious. The missing element is the quiet architecture of incentives, the invisible hand that guides behavior at every level. From the smallest personal decisions to the most complex societal systems, incentives shape what gets done, repeated, and rewarded. This book is a map for seeing those forces clearly and for designing better ones. Whether you are leading a team, raising a family, shaping policy, or building your own future, understanding how to align incentives with desired outcomes is the key to predictable, meaningful results.

Part I — Why Incentives Shape Everything

CHAPTER .1

THE INVISIBLE HAND IS ACTUALLY AN INCENTIVE SYSTEM

Human behavior is far less about character than it is about the rewards and punishments attached to each choice.

The idea of the "invisible hand," popularized by Adam Smith, is often misinterpreted as a mystical force that magically balances markets and society. In reality, the invisible hand is nothing more than the aggregation of countless individual incentives interacting across a system. Every decision people make is influenced by anticipated rewards and penalties, which shape behavior more reliably than moral character or ideology. Businesses thrive not because their leaders are inherently virtuous, but because the system rewards behaviors that increase profit, efficiency, and customer satisfaction. Likewise, failures are usually not a result of poor intentions, but rather of incentives that encourage counterproductive or destructive actions. Understanding this principle is crucial for anyone seeking to influence behavior in organizations, markets, or society at large.

Every human interaction, whether in commerce, governance, or personal relationships, is shaped by incentives. People respond predictably to rewards such as money, recognition, or promotions, and they avoid penalties like fines, demotion, or social disapproval. The invisible hand functions as a natural feedback mechanism, reinforcing behaviors that achieve desired outcomes while discouraging behaviors that fail. By observing patterns in organizations and markets, leaders can trace the incentives that produce them and predict likely outcomes. Incentives are not just tools for controlling behavior; they are the architecture of outcomes. Ignoring them is like designing a building without considering gravity—it may look elegant on paper but will collapse in practice.

Markets are frequently celebrated as models of spontaneous order, but they are guided by a network of incentives. Profit and loss, competition, and customer feedback serve as signals that reward success and penalize failure. Companies that innovate, satisfy clients, and manage resources efficiently prosper because these behaviors are aligned with the system's rewards. Conversely, firms that ignore market signals, mismanage resources, or cut ethical corners fail because the system penalizes them. These principles are not confined to economics; they also apply to politics, healthcare, and education. Incentives provide a predictable framework to understand and influence outcomes across almost every domain of life.

Institutions, including governments and nonprofit organizations, operate under similarly structured incentive systems. Schools may reward teachers for students' standardized test performance rather than for fostering critical thinking. Hospitals may incentivize quantity of procedures rather than patient outcomes. Politicians may prioritize policies that increase re-election chances rather than long-term societal benefit. Even in personal life, choices often reflect immediate gratification over long-term wellness due to the incentives embedded in our environment. By analyzing these patterns, leaders can identify misalignments and design incentives to guide behavior toward desired outcomes.

Recognizing the invisible hand as a system of incentives transforms our approach from passive observation to active design. Leaders and policymakers who understand feedback loops can intentionally shape behaviors to produce predictable and beneficial results. Misaligned incentives can be corrected by restructuring rewards and penalties, thereby influencing choices without coercion. When applied thoughtfully, incentive design can produce sustainable, ethical, and high-impact outcomes that align with organizational or societal goals. The challenge lies in identifying which behaviors to encourage and which to discourage, requiring careful observation, experimentation, and adjustment. Mastering incentives allows individuals and organizations to harness the invisible hand as a tool for predictable success.

Consider how companies use sales commissions as a clear example of incentives at work. A salesperson's behavior is guided less by personal ethics or customer care and more by the compensation structure. When commissions reward volume rather than quality, salespeople may oversell or misrepresent products, creating short-term profit but long-term reputational damage. If the commission structure shifts to reward customer retention and satisfaction, the same salespeople are incentivized to act in ways that genuinely benefit both the customer and the company. The behavior changes not because people have suddenly become more ethical, but because the system's incentives now favor sustainable success. This principle illustrates that the invisible hand functions through the predictable responses to incentives, rather than through abstract morality.

In public policy, the consequences of ignoring incentives are even more apparent. Welfare programs intended to alleviate poverty sometimes unintentionally encourage dependency if benefits are reduced abruptly once recipients achieve moderate income gains. The behavior of recipients is rational: the system penalizes self-sufficiency and rewards stagnation. By redesigning the incentives —for example, gradually tapering benefits while rewarding increased employment—governments can align individual behavior with societal goals. Similarly, tax codes, subsidies, and regulatory policies all carry implicit incentives that shape business decisions, innovation, and social behavior. Leaders who recognize this can predict the secondary effects of policy interventions. Incentives, when overlooked, act invisibly to undermine well-intentioned programs.

Markets, politics, and personal behavior all demonstrate that incentives are stronger than ideology. People often act in ways that contradict their stated beliefs when the rewards and punishments of the system pull them in another direction. For instance, a politician may publicly advocate for environmental protection, yet support policies that benefit industrial donors if the incentives favor short-term political survival. Similarly, employees may espouse teamwork but hoard information when individual recognition or promotion is at stake. Understanding that behavior is shaped more by incentives than intentions allows leaders to design systems that guide people toward aligned outcomes. This predictive power is the practical value of seeing the invisible hand as an incentive system.

The invisible hand also explains the unintended consequences that frequently emerge in complex systems. A company may implement a new productivity metric to encourage efficiency, only to discover employees have learned to game the metric rather than improve outcomes. Hospitals may focus on reducing wait times at the expense of patient care quality. Governments may incentivize reporting of activity rather than results. In every case, the system's incentives produce behavior that was not intended by the designers. These failures are not random—they are predictable results of incentive misalignment. Recognizing this pattern equips leaders to anticipate and correct undesired outcomes before they become systemic problems.

Understanding the invisible hand as an incentive system becomes even clearer when we examine historical examples of organizational and societal behavior. During the Industrial Revolution, factory owners were motivated to maximize output because labor laws and safety regulations were minimal, creating incentives to prioritize speed and profit over worker welfare. This led to widespread exploitation, unsafe working conditions, and high mortality rates—outcomes no one would intentionally design today. Governments eventually intervened, creating labor standards and safety incentives, which changed behavior across entire industries. The system shifted from rewarding short-term exploitation to rewarding safe, sustainable practices, showing that redesigning incentives can dramatically improve societal outcomes. This example demonstrates that incentives, rather than abstract morality or ideology, drive systemic change. By studying these patterns, modern leaders can apply similar principles to contemporary challenges.

Corporate culture provides another compelling example of incentives at work. Consider a technology company that rewards employees solely based on individual performance metrics, such as lines of code or closed deals. Such incentives often encourage competition over collaboration, creating an environment where knowledge hoarding and sabotage are common. When the company adjusts its incentive structure to value teamwork, mentorship, and shared project success, employee behavior shifts to align with organizational goals. Rewards and recognition now reinforce cooperative behavior, innovation, and long-term productivity. This case illustrates that even deeply ingrained workplace habits can be reshaped by realigning incentives. Leaders who understand this can influence corporate culture without relying on abstract moral appeals or force.

The financial industry offers yet another lens through which to view the invisible hand. Before the 2008 financial crisis, many banks incentivized short-term profits through large bonuses for risky investments, without penalizing long-term losses or ethical violations. As a result, employees made decisions that benefited themselves in the short term but ultimately destabilized global markets. After the crisis, regulatory changes and revised compensation structures aimed to reward sustainable growth and risk management. This shift demonstrates that even in complex, high-stakes systems, incentives dictate behavior far more than ideals or ethics. Understanding the feedback loops in such systems allows regulators and corporate leaders to predict and influence outcomes more effectively. The invisible hand is not passive; it reacts predictably to the incentives embedded within it.

Even at the individual level, incentives shape behavior in ways most people fail to recognize. Consider personal finance: individuals may accumulate high-interest debt not because of irresponsibility but because the system makes short-term consumption more rewarding than long-term saving. Credit card offers, promotional sales, and instant gratification reward immediate spending, while the consequences of debt accumulate slowly. By redesigning personal incentives—such as automatic savings, investment matching, or debt repayment rewards—individuals can align behavior with long-term goals. The principle is the same across organizations and governments: outcomes follow the incentives, not the intentions. Recognizing this allows individuals to design environments in which good behavior is easier than bad behavior. Incentives, therefore, are the hidden architecture of our personal and professional lives.

Finally, mastering the invisible hand as an incentive system requires deliberate observation and thoughtful experimentation. Leaders, managers, and policymakers must first map out existing incentives and the behaviors they produce, identifying misalignments that generate unintended consequences. They can then design or adjust incentives to promote desired actions while discouraging harmful ones. This process is iterative; systems must be monitored, measured, and refined continuously to maintain alignment with long-term goals. When executed effectively, incentive redesign can transform organizations, societies, and individual lives in measurable, positive ways. The invisible hand, once understood, ceases to be a mysterious force and becomes a practical tool for shaping predictable, beneficial outcomes. By thinking systematically about incentives, we gain the ability to guide behavior toward success, sustainability, and ethical integrity.

CHAPTER .2

GOOD PEOPLE DO BAD THINGS UNDER BAD INCENTIVES

Misaligned incentives routinely push ethical individuals toward harmful outcomes they never intended.

Even the most ethical individuals can act in harmful ways when the system rewards the wrong behaviors. Human behavior is highly sensitive to the consequences attached to actions, often more so than to moral reasoning or values. In organizations, employees may cut corners, misreport results, or prioritize personal gain if such behavior is compensated or left unpunished. In government, officials may support inefficient or corrupt programs if political survival or public praise is tied to superficial metrics. Even in everyday life, people often make decisions that benefit themselves in the short term while harming others in the long term. Understanding the mechanisms that push good people toward bad outcomes is essential for designing systems that produce positive behavior.

One classic example of misaligned incentives comes from the banking and financial sector. Prior to the 2008 financial crisis, traders and executives were rewarded heavily for short-term profits with little accountability for long-term losses. Many otherwise competent and ethical individuals participated in risky behavior because the incentives favored immediate gains. The systemic rewards overshadowed personal ethics, illustrating that context can override morality when outcomes are tied to measurable compensation. Post-crisis reforms attempted to redesign these incentives by linking bonuses to long-term performance, risk management, and ethical compliance. This example shows that even in highly professional environments, bad incentives can make good people act destructively without ill intent. Systems, not individuals alone, create behaviors.

In corporate settings beyond finance, misaligned incentives frequently undermine innovation and collaboration. Consider a software development company that rewards only speed of delivery rather than quality or team cooperation. Developers may cut corners, skip testing, or avoid helping colleagues because the incentive structure rewards rapid completion over sustainable solutions. The individuals involved are not lazy or malicious; they are simply responding rationally to the rewards offered. Adjusting the incentives—such as rewarding code quality, mentorship, and cross-team collaboration—changes behavior without changing the people themselves. Good employees perform poorly only when the system fails to guide them toward constructive behavior. Aligning incentives with desired outcomes is therefore a strategic imperative for leaders.

Government programs and public policy also illustrate the power of bad incentives to distort behavior. Welfare systems, healthcare reimbursement schemes, or education funding models often unintentionally reward compliance with rules rather than achievement of outcomes. For example, schools may focus on "teaching to the test" because standardized test performance is the metric that drives funding and recognition. Doctors may over-prescribe tests or treatments because the system pays for quantity, not patient wellness. Civil servants may prioritize bureaucratic survival over innovative solutions if promotions depend on paperwork rather than impact. In each case, the individuals involved are acting rationally within the incentive structures, not because they are unethical. Redesigning the incentives can redirect good intentions into genuinely productive outcomes.

Even at the personal level, misaligned incentives shape everyday decisions. Employees may stay in unfulfilling jobs that pay more because immediate financial rewards outweigh long-term career satisfaction. Consumers may over consume, take on debt, or neglect health because instant gratification is incentivized, while delayed consequences are weakly felt. Parents may prioritize tasks that yield visible praise over long-term family wellbeing because recognition feels rewarding. By consciously adjusting personal incentive structures—such as automating savings, rewarding learning, or measuring progress toward long-term goals—individuals can align behavior with their values. Understanding how misaligned incentives work allows people to avoid common traps that lead them to act against their own interests or ethics. Ultimately, behavior reflects the system more than the individual.

Even strong ethical cultures in organizations can be undermined by poorly designed incentive systems. For example, in sales-driven environments, employees may exaggerate results or mislead customers to hit quotas if bonuses depend solely on short-term performance. Leaders often assume that moral employees will resist unethical shortcuts, but behavior is overwhelmingly shaped by the structure of rewards and penalties. Research in behavioral economics shows that even minor financial incentives can shift decision-making, sometimes overpowering deeply held ethical beliefs. Adjusting the incentive system to reward transparency, long-term client relationships, and teamwork can guide employees toward ethical behavior naturally. This demonstrates that good people do not need to be "controlled"; they need the system to support the right choices.

Historical examples further illustrate how incentives can override morality on a massive scale. During the Prohibition era in the United States, law enforcement officers and politicians were faced with conflicting incentives. Bribes, political pressure, and public attention rewarded overlooking illegal alcohol production and distribution, despite the legal and ethical standards they swore to uphold. Many individuals who might have been law-abiding in other contexts became complicit in illegal activities because the incentives favored compliance with corruption over enforcement of the law. The consequences included organized crime growth and widespread societal harm, showing that incentive structures can reshape collective behavior. Correcting such misalignments requires not only legal enforcement but also redesigning reward systems to align ethics with tangible benefits. Understanding these dynamics allows policymakers to prevent well-intentioned individuals from being pushed into harmful actions.

In corporate governance, misaligned incentives have repeatedly caused ethical lapses and systemic failure. The Enron scandal, for instance, was fueled by executive compensation schemes that rewarded short-term stock performance rather than sustainable profitability. Employees engaged in accounting fraud and deceptive reporting, not because they lacked skill or morality, but because the system rewarded manipulation over integrity. When incentives prioritize outcomes disconnected from reality or ethics, even competent and principled people can make choices they would otherwise consider wrong. Corrective measures, such as linking bonuses to long-term performance and ethical compliance, reduce the likelihood of such outcomes. Leaders must recognize that responsibility for ethical behavior often lies more in the design of incentives than in policing character. Designing systems that inherently reward integrity is a more effective strategy than relying on oversight alone.

Misaligned incentives also distort decision-making in public health and social services. Doctors may over-prescribe medications, hospitals may prioritize procedures over preventative care, and social workers may focus on paperwork compliance rather than client outcomes—all because the system rewards measurable actions rather than results. Individuals within these systems are generally motivated by a desire to help, yet the incentives inadvertently steer them toward outcomes that are suboptimal or even harmful. Adjusting incentive structures to reward outcomes rather than inputs, such as patient recovery or client independence, can dramatically improve results without changing the people involved. This highlights the power of incentives to channel ethical intentions into positive outcomes. By realigning rewards and penalties with desired results, organizations can prevent unintentional harm caused by well-meaning individuals.

Even in everyday personal behavior, incentives strongly influence decisions that might otherwise contradict values. For instance, individuals may procrastinate on long-term health goals, education, or financial planning because immediate gratification is consistently rewarded, while delayed benefits feel intangible. Automating positive incentives, such as setting up savings plans, rewarding milestones in skill development, or using accountability systems for health goals, can reshape behavior to align with long-term intentions. Parents, teachers, and leaders can use the same principle by designing environments that naturally reward ethical, productive, and constructive behavior. Understanding that good people act poorly under bad incentives empowers leaders to design systems that guide behavior toward collective benefit. Ultimately, the path to sustainable ethical behavior lies in reshaping the environment, not solely appealing to personal virtue.

Even minor adjustments in incentive structures can prevent ethical lapses before they occur. For example, organizations that tie team bonuses to collective outcomes rather than individual metrics see a reduction in selfish behavior and a rise in cooperation. Governments that design social programs with gradual benefits and positive reinforcement reduce dependency and increase self-sufficiency. By anticipating how people respond to rewards and penalties, leaders can avoid creating conditions that unintentionally encourage unethical or counterproductive actions. Psychology studies consistently show that people respond more reliably to immediate, tangible incentives than to abstract moral imperatives. Leaders who design incentives intentionally create systems in which doing the right thing becomes the easiest and most rewarding choice. This strategic approach minimizes moral conflict and maximizes organizational and societal benefit.

Educational systems often reveal the unintended consequences of poorly aligned incentives. Schools that reward only test scores inadvertently encourage teachers and students to focus narrowly on examination performance rather than holistic learning. Cheating scandals, teaching to the test, and stress-related issues arise because the incentive structure values the wrong outcome. By redesigning incentives to reward creativity, critical thinking, and engagement, schools can align student and teacher behavior with long-term educational goals. Ethical individuals within the system respond predictably to the rewards available; misalignment, not character flaws, is usually the root cause of failure. This principle applies across sectors: misaligned incentives explain why well-intentioned people sometimes produce harmful results. Recognizing this empowers leaders to craft systems that produce consistent, positive outcomes.

Corporate compliance programs illustrate another dimension of incentive misalignment. Organizations often invest in ethical codes and training programs but fail to change the reward structures that drive behavior. Employees may understand what is "right" but face promotion or bonus systems that incentivize cutting corners, meeting quotas, or hiding errors. The result is predictable: ethical lapses occur even among competent, well-meaning staff. By linking rewards to both outcomes and ethical adherence, companies create an environment where doing the right thing is rational and profitable. Misalignment, therefore, is the primary driver of unethical actions, not the absence of morality. Well-designed incentives prevent the need for policing, auditing, or coercion to enforce ethical behavior.

Finally, leaders can apply these lessons proactively to prevent ethical failures before they occur. Mapping the incentive landscape, identifying misalignments, and redesigning rewards and penalties ensures that systems naturally guide behavior toward the desired outcomes. This approach works across all levels: corporate, governmental, educational, and personal. When good people are placed in environments where the incentives support constructive behavior, their ethical intentions align with observable results. Recognizing that "good people do bad things under bad incentives" is the first step toward building systems that channel talent and morality into sustainable success. Mastering this principle empowers leaders to create cultures, policies, and practices where doing the right thing is the default and the rewarded behavior.

CHAPTER .3

INCENTIVES EXPLAIN MORE THAN IDEOLOGY EVER COULD

Most political, economic, and social conflicts persist because incentives overpower beliefs.

Many conflicts that appear to be rooted in ideology are actually driven by incentives that shape behavior in predictable ways. People often justify actions with beliefs or principles, but their choices are heavily influenced by the rewards and penalties present in the system around them. Politicians may champion policies that contradict their stated ideals if doing so maximizes votes, funding, or personal advancement. Employees may act against company values if bonus structures reward short-term gains over ethical or long-term objectives. Understanding incentives allows leaders to predict behavior more reliably than analyzing beliefs alone. Systems, rather than ideologies, are often the true drivers of human behavior.

In economics, incentives frequently explain market phenomena that ideology alone cannot. For example, firms may resist environmental regulations not because they reject sustainability, but because compliance is costly under current reward structures. Conversely, companies often innovate in green technologies when subsidies, tax incentives, or consumer demand align economic rewards with ecological goals. Individuals and organizations respond rationally to the incentives they face, sometimes producing results that contradict stated beliefs or moral positions. Recognizing this pattern helps policymakers craft interventions that achieve intended outcomes, rather than relying on appeals to ethics or ideology. Behavior becomes predictable once incentives are mapped and understood. Incentives, therefore, offer a more practical lens for understanding economic decision-making than ideology.

Political behavior is another area where incentives outweigh ideology. Legislators often vote against policies that align with their professed principles if doing so threatens reelection or access to political resources. Party loyalty, donor influence, and electoral calculations create powerful incentives that shape actions more strongly than philosophical beliefs. Similarly, bureaucrats implement policies in ways that maximize career security, departmental budgets, or professional recognition, sometimes contradicting the stated mission of their agencies. These patterns are not evidence of moral failure but of rational responses to incentive structures. By designing political and bureaucratic systems with aligned incentives, societies can encourage behavior that matches both individual intentions and collective goals. Ideology alone is rarely sufficient to drive systemic change.

Corporations demonstrate the same dynamic: employees and executives frequently act contrary to corporate values if incentives reward different outcomes. A company may espouse customer-centric principles, but if performance metrics emphasize short-term sales or cost-cutting, employees will focus on those measures instead. Misalignment between stated values and incentives explains why ethical corporate cultures often struggle to materialize. Conversely, when companies align incentives with desired behavior—such as rewarding customer satisfaction, collaboration, and innovation—values are reinforced naturally. This illustrates that incentives, not ideology, predict day-to-day decisions. Leaders who understand this can design systems that reliably produce aligned outcomes across organizations.

Even at the personal level, incentives often override expressed beliefs or intentions. Individuals may intend to save money, exercise, or eat healthily, yet consistently make choices that contradict these goals when immediate rewards or penalties dominate decision-making. For example, the instant gratification of spending on luxury items can overpower long-term financial planning, even for those ideologically committed to frugality. By structuring personal incentives—automatic savings, progress tracking, or rewarding incremental achievements—people can align behavior with values more effectively than by relying on willpower alone. Understanding the dominance of incentives over ideology empowers individuals to design environments that support consistent action. Predictable behavior emerges when systems reward desired outcomes.

Historical conflicts often reveal the power of incentives over belief. In revolutions, wars, and social movements, individuals may publicly espouse ideological positions while privately acting in self-interest when incentives favor survival, wealth, or influence. Soldiers, bureaucrats, and citizens often make pragmatic decisions that contradict their declared principles because incentives guide risk, reward, and security. By examining the incentive structures present in these situations, historians and policymakers can explain behavior more accurately than by analyzing ideology alone. Aligning incentives with desired outcomes reduces the gap between beliefs and actions, creating stability and predictable success. Incentives, not ideology, are the invisible force that shapes human behavior at scale.

Even well-intentioned corporate leaders can see ideology fail when incentives dominate behavior. A company may declare a commitment to sustainability and ethical sourcing, yet employees and managers may prioritize quarterly revenue or cost-cutting over environmental responsibility. For instance, suppliers may be pushed to meet price and delivery targets even at the expense of labor standards or ecological compliance. The leadership's values alone cannot override the incentive structure driving day-to-day decisions. By aligning rewards—bonuses, promotions, recognition—with sustainable and ethical outcomes, companies ensure that employees act in ways consistent with corporate ideals. This demonstrates that predictable behavior is achieved not through persuasion or ideology but through the careful design of incentive systems.

In government and public policy, misaligned incentives often explain why good ideas fail despite widespread support. Consider environmental legislation: elected officials may publicly endorse green initiatives, yet vote against effective regulations when political or financial incentives favor industrial stakeholders or short-term economic growth. Similarly, bureaucrats may implement programs in ways that secure departmental budgets rather than achieving intended social outcomes. Citizens may support policies in principle but act contrary to them when tax benefits, subsidies, or penalties favor alternative behavior. These examples illustrate that the incentive structure often outweighs ideology in determining practical outcomes. Policy design that ignores these incentive dynamics risks repeated failure regardless of noble intentions.

Historical conflicts and revolutions further underscore the primacy of incentives over ideology. In periods of political upheaval, soldiers and citizens often make decisions based on personal safety, resource access, or social standing rather than ideological loyalty. During the French Revolution, for example, many individuals publicly professed revolutionary ideals while privately aligning with counter-revolutionary factions when it served personal survival or advantage. Similarly, bureaucrats in various regimes have historically implemented policies to protect careers rather than uphold ethical or ideological commitments. These behaviors are rational responses to the prevailing incentive structures. By understanding the rewards and penalties embedded in such systems, historians and policymakers can explain actions more reliably than by analyzing stated beliefs alone.

Nonprofit and social sector organizations also highlight how incentives drive behavior beyond ideology. Charitable organizations may declare a mission of community development, yet employees often focus on fundraising targets and donor relations because success is measured in dollars raised rather than community impact. Volunteers and staff may inadvertently prioritize visibility over effectiveness if recognition or advancement is tied to high-profile campaigns rather than outcomes. By restructuring incentives to reward measurable social impact, nonprofits can guide behavior toward achieving their stated mission. This demonstrates that even in altruistic organizations, ideology without aligned incentives fails to produce consistent results. Designing effective incentives ensures that values translate into action.

On the individual level, incentives explain behavior that ideology alone cannot predict. People may espouse frugality, health consciousness, or lifelong learning, yet succumb to behaviors that contradict these ideals when immediate rewards are stronger. For example, someone committed to healthy living may indulge in junk food if social approval or convenience offers a greater reward. Students may value education but procrastinate when the system rewards last-minute performance or test-focused outcomes. By structuring personal incentives—such as progress tracking, milestone rewards, or accountability mechanisms—individuals can align day-to-day actions with long-term goals. Understanding the primacy of incentives enables predictable behavior without relying on abstract willpower. In all domains, the design of reward and penalty structures consistently explains actions better than ideology alone.

Corporate scandals demonstrate the practical consequences of failing to align incentives with ideology. The Volkswagen emissions scandal illustrates how employees acted against environmental and corporate values because management incentives prioritized market share and financial targets over compliance. Engineers and managers complied with unethical practices because doing so rewarded immediate success and avoided penalties, despite conflicting with personal and corporate ideals. When incentives were later adjusted, including regulatory penalties and oversight mechanisms, behavior shifted, reinforcing ethical compliance. Similarly, in finance, traders took excessive risks during the 2008 crisis because short-term profits were rewarded more than long-term stability or ethical considerations.

These examples show that predictable results emerge when incentive structures are understood and addressed. Ideology without supportive incentives is insufficient to guide consistent behavior.

Even in democratic societies, incentives frequently outweigh political ideology in shaping outcomes. Voters often prioritize candidates who promise short-term economic or social benefits rather than those aligned with ideological consistency. Politicians, in turn, adjust policy proposals to secure votes, campaign donations, or media attention, sometimes contradicting their stated beliefs. Bureaucrats may implement policies in ways that maximize career advancement, budget security, or institutional influence rather than ideological adherence. Understanding these incentives allows citizens, policymakers, and activists to predict behavior and design interventions that achieve intended outcomes. By aligning rewards with desired behavior, societies can close the gap between ideology and action. Incentives, therefore, are a more practical tool than belief systems for achieving meaningful results.

Finally, leaders can harness the dominance of incentives over ideology to create systems that consistently produce desired outcomes. Mapping the incentive landscape and identifying misalignments allows organizations, governments, and individuals to anticipate behavior before it occurs. Incentives can then be deliberately structured so that doing the right thing is also the most rewarding choice. Whether in corporate ethics, public policy, or personal development, this approach aligns values, goals, and behavior for sustainable success. Ideology without proper incentives is often powerless to produce predictable action, whereas well-designed incentives guide behavior automatically. By recognizing that incentives explain more than ideology ever could, leaders gain a reliable framework for shaping human behavior at all levels.

Chapter .4

What Gets Rewarded Gets Repeated

Systems always produce more of whatever behavior they compensate, regardless of stated values.

Behavior is rarely random; it responds to the signals embedded within systems. When certain actions are rewarded, individuals and organizations naturally repeat them, often without conscious thought. Conversely, behaviors that are ignored or penalized tend to disappear, regardless of their inherent value or alignment with stated goals. This principle explains why organizations and societies often produce outcomes that contradict their declared values. Ethical conduct, innovation, cooperation, or long-term thinking will flourish only if they are systematically rewarded. Recognizing this fundamental law of behavior allows leaders to intentionally shape patterns of action toward desired results.

In corporate environments, the principle that "what gets rewarded gets repeated" manifests daily. Sales teams rewarded purely for volume may prioritize quantity over quality, damaging customer relationships and long-term brand value. Conversely, companies that reward customer retention, collaboration, and innovation see those behaviors increase naturally. Leaders cannot simply declare desired values; they must embed them into the reward structure. Bonuses, promotions, recognition, and career growth must align with the behaviors the organization wants to amplify. When incentives reflect stated values, employees naturally act in ways that reinforce the culture and organizational mission.

Government and policy systems also illustrate this dynamic. Agencies often emphasize procedural compliance or short-term metrics, incentivizing activity rather than meaningful outcomes. For example, schools focusing solely on standardized test scores may see teaching to the test increase while critical thinking and creativity decline. Social programs that reward reporting over results often produce paperwork compliance rather than social impact. Leaders who redesign incentives to reward real outcomes —like student mastery, health improvements, or reduced recidivism—align behavior with intended goals. By shaping what is rewarded, governments can ensure that actions follow mission rather than bureaucracy. Incentive design, therefore, is a central lever for systemic effectiveness.

Historical examples demonstrate that societies also reflect the behaviors they reward. In the Roman Empire, landowners and officials were often rewarded for visible wealth accumulation and military success rather than public welfare or civic virtue. Over time, this reinforced behaviors that prioritized personal gain and conquest over societal stability. Similarly, in modern corporate or political systems, visible achievements—like quarterly profit, headline-making policies, or award recognition—are often rewarded at the expense of long-term health or ethical consistency. Societies and organizations inevitably replicate the behaviors they incentivize. Leaders who wish to promote ethical, sustainable, and cooperative behavior must structure rewards to make those actions more frequent and visible.

Even at the individual level, the principle is powerful. Habits, productivity, and personal growth are reinforced by reward mechanisms, whether intrinsic or extrinsic. People naturally repeat actions that produce satisfaction, recognition, or tangible benefits, and abandon those that go unrewarded or produce discomfort. For instance, employees may work overtime if promotions, bonuses, or praise are tied to visible effort, regardless of actual productivity. Conversely, habits like continuous learning, collaboration, or wellness thrive when small rewards consistently reinforce the behavior. By understanding which behaviors are amplified by incentives, individuals can engineer environments that naturally encourage desirable habits. Predictable outcomes emerge when leaders and individuals align rewards with the behaviors they want to see repeated.

Corporate case studies further illustrate this principle. A technology company might initially reward engineers for shipping features quickly, but over time, quality issues and bugs accumulate because speed was the rewarded behavior. Adjusting incentives to reward user satisfaction, code quality, and innovation changes behavior across the organization without coercion. Similarly, nonprofit organizations may reward fundraising success over mission impact, inadvertently distorting priorities. By realigning rewards with outcomes, behavior shifts in a predictable and positive direction. Leaders who grasp that "what gets rewarded gets repeated" gain a powerful tool to shape both culture and results. Incentives are not abstract—they are the primary mechanism through which behavior is replicated and sustained.

Even small, carefully targeted rewards can have disproportionate effects. Recognition programs, milestone bonuses, or public acknowledgment can shift organizational behavior significantly when structured thoughtfully. Governments, for instance, may encourage energy efficiency by providing tax credits, subsidies, or public awards for sustainable practices. Employees may embrace innovation when their creative contributions are celebrated and rewarded, not just penalized for mistakes. By focusing on the behaviors they want to see more frequently, leaders can create a self-reinforcing cycle of improvement. Conversely, rewarding the wrong behaviors—even unintentionally—produces repeated mistakes, inefficiency, and ethical lapses. Understanding this principle allows leaders to direct repeated actions toward organizational, societal, and personal goals.

Education systems also demonstrate this effect vividly. When teachers and students are rewarded solely for grades, rote memorization and test-focused instruction increase. Critical thinking, problem-solving, and creative inquiry often decline because these behaviors are not recognized or rewarded. Systems that reward curiosity, mastery, and engagement naturally produce more of these behaviors, reinforcing the desired culture of learning. Students and educators respond predictably to what is incentivized, regardless of stated values. By carefully aligning rewards with intended outcomes, school leaders ensure that desired behaviors are repeated consistently. Predictable behavior flows from well-designed systems, not moral exhortation alone.

Finally, understanding that "what gets rewarded gets repeated" empowers leaders to proactively design systems for success. Every action, whether at the individual, organizational, or societal level, is influenced by the incentives present. Misalignment between stated values and actual rewards creates persistent inefficiency, ethical lapses, and undesired behavior. Aligning incentives with desired outcomes ensures that behaviors reinforcing success, sustainability, and ethics are naturally repeated. Leaders can leverage this principle to create cultures, policies, and personal habits that reliably produce positive results. Recognizing and intentionally shaping incentives transforms environments into self-reinforcing systems of achievement.

CHAPTER .5

THE DIFFERENCE BETWEEN INTENTIONS AND OUTCOMES IS INCENTIVES

Well-meaning policies fail when incentives contradict their stated goals.

Good intentions alone rarely produce good outcomes. People, organizations, and governments may act with the best of motives, yet the results often diverge sharply from their aims. The missing link is incentives: the structure of rewards and penalties that shape behavior and drive results. When incentives contradict stated objectives, even ethical, skilled, and well-intentioned actors can produce harmful or unintended consequences. Policies, corporate strategies, and social programs fail not because of incompetence, but because the systems guiding behavior reward the wrong actions. Understanding how incentives bridge—or break—the connection between intention and outcome is critical for effective leadership.

Corporate examples illustrate this principle vividly. Consider a company that promotes a culture of customer satisfaction but bases employee bonuses solely on sales volume. Staff may aggressively push products, exaggerate benefits, or neglect after-sales support, producing outcomes that conflict with the company's stated values. The intentions were positive—providing excellent service—but the incentives encouraged behaviors that undermined those goals. Changing the reward structure to value customer retention, satisfaction scores, and problem resolution aligns actions with intentions. Similarly, innovation programs may fail when risk-taking is penalized even as creative thinking is encouraged verbally. Incentives determine which behaviors are repeated, making them the bridge between intention and outcome.

Governments and policymakers face similar challenges. Well-intentioned social programs often fail when the incentive structure rewards compliance over results. For instance, unemployment benefits may unintentionally discourage job-seeking if recipients lose support too quickly upon gaining employment. Schools may reward standardized test performance rather than actual learning, producing high scores without improved critical thinking. Health programs may compensate quantity of treatment over patient recovery, incentivizing overuse of procedures without improving outcomes. In each case, the system rewards the wrong actions, undermining well-meaning intentions. Redesigning incentives ensures that good intentions translate into tangible, positive results.

Even personal development efforts are shaped by incentives. Individuals may intend to save money, exercise regularly, or improve their skills, but without mechanisms that reward these behaviors, intentions often fail. A person may plan to exercise but skip workouts because immediate comfort is unconsciously rewarded, while delayed benefits remain abstract. Similarly, someone may want to learn a new skill but avoid practice when the system of incentives favors instant gratification or visible social approval. By structuring personal rewards—progress tracking, milestone celebrations, or habit streaks—individuals align daily actions with long-term goals. The difference between what people intend and what they actually accomplish is often the incentives embedded in their environment.

Historical and social examples further highlight this principle. Colonial administrations frequently implemented reforms with benevolent intentions, yet outcomes often exacerbated inequality or inefficiency. Local officials responded rationally to the incentives in the system, which prioritized revenue extraction, political stability, or career advancement over the intended social good. Similarly, corporate scandals often occur when leaders' ethical intentions clash with incentive structures that reward short-term profits or visibility over long-term sustainability. In both cases, outcomes diverged sharply from intentions because the system shaped behavior. Recognizing the role of incentives allows leaders to predict, prevent, and correct misaligned results before they become systemic problems.

Aligning incentives with intended outcomes requires deliberate design. Leaders must first map the existing reward and penalty structures and identify points where behavior diverges from desired goals. Adjustments can include redesigning performance metrics, modifying compensation, or restructuring feedback loops. In government, this might involve tying funding to measurable impact rather than activity alone. In corporations, it could mean rewarding quality, collaboration, and long-term value creation rather than only short-term achievements. On a personal level, habit tracking, progress rewards, and accountability partners serve as incentive mechanisms that align actions with intentions. When incentives are properly aligned, intentions and outcomes converge, producing predictable, ethical, and effective results.

Even small incentive misalignments can produce disproportionately large divergences between intention and outcome. A minor misalignment in metrics, compensation, or recognition can amplify over time, creating systemic inefficiencies or unintended consequences. For example, a company that rewards customer acquisition without retention may see initial growth but long-term churn and reputational damage. Similarly, policy programs that reward reporting over results may produce mountains of paperwork without measurable improvement. By proactively analyzing and aligning incentives, leaders can prevent these cascading negative effects. Incentive design is the critical lever that transforms well-meaning intentions into meaningful outcomes.

Corporate governance illustrates this principle at scale. Executive bonuses tied to short-term stock performance rather than sustainable growth often lead to risky decisions, ethical lapses, or accounting manipulation. The intentions may be to grow the company and create shareholder value, but incentives create behaviors that undermine long-term stability. Boards that redesign incentives to include ethical compliance, long-term profitability, and stakeholder satisfaction align executives' actions with organizational objectives. Employees, in turn, respond predictably to the rewards and penalties they encounter daily. Aligning intentions and outcomes through incentives is therefore both a strategic and ethical imperative. Properly designed systems produce behaviors that consistently reflect stated values.

Even in education, incentives shape whether students and teachers achieve intended outcomes. If schools reward only test scores, teachers teach to the test and students memorize answers, producing high grades but little understanding. Adjusting incentives to reward mastery, creativity, and critical thinking ensures that the daily actions of teachers and students align with educational goals. Similar principles apply in healthcare, public administration, and social services, where outcomes diverge from intentions unless behavior is guided by aligned incentives. Leaders who neglect this principle are left blaming individuals or ideology for systemic failures. Understanding and designing incentives is the practical key to converting intentions into results.

Finally, mastering the connection between incentives, intentions, and outcomes empowers leaders at every level. Well-intentioned actions, policies, and strategies will only succeed if the surrounding system rewards behaviors that produce the desired results. By mapping incentives, identifying misalignments, and redesigning rewards and penalties, leaders can ensure that ethical intentions, strategic goals, and practical actions converge. Systems become self-reinforcing, predictable, and effective, transforming good intentions into measurable achievements. Incentives are the bridge between what we hope to achieve and what actually happens. Recognizing and designing for this principle is essential for sustainable success in business, policy, and personal life.

Part II — The Hidden Incentive Traps We Live In

CHAPTER .6

SHORT-TERM REWARDS ARE DESTROYING LONG-TERM THINKING

Modern systems prioritize immediate gains at the expense of sustainable outcomes.

Short-term incentives dominate much of modern decision-making, often at the expense of long-term goals. Companies, governments, and individuals frequently prioritize immediate benefits, rewards, or recognition while ignoring the cumulative consequences of their actions. This focus on instant gratification produces predictable but often harmful outcomes, such as environmental degradation, financial instability, or health decline. Short-term rewards distort priorities, encouraging behaviors that maximize immediate gain rather than sustainable value. Understanding this dynamic is essential for designing systems that balance present needs with future success. Leaders who fail to account for the effects of short-term incentives risk undermining long-term strategy and well-being.

In the corporate world, quarterly reporting and performance bonuses are prime examples of short-term thinking. Executives may make decisions that boost stock prices temporarily, cut essential research, or defer maintenance to meet short-term targets. While these actions produce immediate recognition or profit, they often compromise long-term stability, innovation, and competitiveness. Companies that reward sustainable growth, customer loyalty, and ethical practices align immediate actions with future success. This requires redesigning metrics and incentive structures to emphasize outcomes over transient achievements. Leaders who can balance short-term wins with long-term vision produce more resilient and thriving organizations.

Government policies are similarly affected by short-term incentives. Politicians often prioritize initiatives that deliver visible results within election cycles rather than sustainable solutions. Infrastructure projects, social programs, and regulatory reforms are frequently designed to provide immediate wins rather than lasting benefits. Bureaucrats may focus on meeting yearly performance metrics or budget targets instead of addressing systemic issues. By realigning incentives to reward long-term outcomes, governments can ensure that decisions today do not undermine future prosperity. Sustainable policy design requires a deliberate balance between immediate action and long-term consequences.

Even in personal development, short-term rewards often override long-term planning. Individuals may prioritize activities that provide instant satisfaction, such as spending money impulsively, skipping workouts, or procrastinating learning goals. These behaviors feel rational in the present because the rewards are immediate and tangible, while the benefits of long-term planning remain abstract or delayed. Personal systems can be redesigned by introducing mechanisms that reward incremental progress, milestone achievements, or delayed gratification. Tools like habit tracking, accountability partners, and progress visualization align daily actions with long-term objectives. Understanding the tension between short-term incentives and long-term success is critical for achieving meaningful personal growth.

Historical examples highlight the destructive potential of prioritizing short-term gains. Industrial expansion in the 19th and 20th centuries often produced immediate profits while exhausting natural resources and harming communities. Financial markets regularly experience speculative bubbles when short-term profit incentives overshadow prudent, long-term investment. Even civilizations have declined because leadership prioritized immediate reward or conquest at the expense of long-term sustainability. These patterns illustrate a universal truth: systems that overemphasize short-term rewards erode future stability and growth. Recognizing this dynamic allows leaders to create structures that encourage sustainable, forward-thinking behavior while still acknowledging present needs.

Corporate innovation suffers under short-term incentive structures. R&D teams may abandon ambitious projects because the payoff is long-term and uncertain, while immediate performance metrics dominate evaluation. Companies that design incentives to reward experimentation, learning, and long-term value creation see greater innovation and resilience. This approach requires patience, trust in processes, and a willingness to prioritize outcomes over output speed. Organizations that successfully balance short-term achievement with long-term investment outperform those that chase instant rewards alone. Leaders must cultivate a culture that values foresight as much as performance to sustain growth.

Financial systems are particularly sensitive to short-termism. Traders, executives, and investors often focus on quarterly results, short-term profits, and market optics rather than sustainable financial health. The 2008 financial crisis provides a stark illustration of the consequences: immediate profit incentives encouraged excessive risk-taking, while the long-term systemic consequences were catastrophic. By restructuring incentives to reward stability, risk management, and long-term value creation, financial institutions can align daily behavior with sustainable outcomes. Understanding the influence of short-term incentives allows leaders to design safer, more resilient financial systems. Incentive architecture can prevent individual rationality from producing collective harm.

In government and environmental policy, the tension between short-term and long-term incentives is evident. Climate change mitigation, infrastructure resilience, and public health planning often suffer because immediate political rewards are limited. Legislators may prioritize policies that yield instant popularity while deferring investments in sustainable solutions. Long-term planning requires mechanisms that reward foresight, consistency, and proactive problem-solving. Tax incentives, subsidies for sustainable practices, and regulatory frameworks can shift focus from immediate benefits to lasting impact. Leaders who design for long-term outcomes create societies capable of thriving across decades, not just election cycles.

Finally, overcoming the dominance of short-term rewards requires conscious system design. Organizations, governments, and individuals must identify where immediate incentives conflict with future goals. Metrics, rewards, and recognition should be adjusted to align short-term behavior with long-term vision. Leaders should cultivate cultures that value delayed gratification, strategic thinking, and forward-looking decision-making. By doing so, systems transform from reactive, short-sighted structures into proactive engines for sustainable success. Recognizing and correcting the imbalance between immediate rewards and long-term outcomes ensures that present actions support enduring progress rather than undermine it.

Chapter .7

Metrics Have Replaced Meaning

When measurements become targets, they stop measuring what actually matters.

Modern organizations, governments, and even personal systems often fall into the trap of measuring what is easy rather than what is meaningful. Metrics are intended to provide insight, guide decisions, and track progress toward important goals. However, when metrics become the ultimate target, they distort behavior, encourage gaming, and produce outcomes that misalign with underlying purpose. Employees focus on hitting numbers rather than achieving real results, leaders prioritize visible indicators over substantive progress, and individuals pursue measurable accomplishments at the expense of personal growth. This phenomenon, known as Good hart's Law, shows that once a measure becomes a target, it ceases to be a reliable indicator. Understanding this principle is essential for designing incentive structures that truly reflect values and goals.

In business, the replacement of meaning with metrics is pervasive. Sales teams may be rewarded for closing deals regardless of customer satisfaction, retention, or long-term relationships. Marketing departments may focus on clicks, impressions, or downloads instead of engagement or brand loyalty. Companies often celebrate growth in vanity metrics while neglecting underlying health, efficiency, or ethical considerations. Employees respond rationally to the rewards tied to these numbers, even if the outcomes undermine the organization's stated mission. Aligning metrics with real value creation ensures that measurable achievements support strategic goals rather than undermine them. Leaders must constantly evaluate whether the metrics they use reflect genuine success or just superficial indicators.

Government and public policy are equally susceptible. Education systems often measure teacher performance by standardized test scores rather than student understanding or critical thinking. Social programs may emphasize reporting compliance instead of measurable improvement in outcomes like health, employment, or well-being. Policymakers respond predictably to these metrics because funding, recognition, and career advancement are tied to them. The focus on numbers rather than meaningful change can produce unintended consequences, such as teaching to the test, bureaucratic inefficiency, or short-term policy wins that fail to address systemic problems. By redesigning metrics to reflect the true outcomes of interest, governments can ensure that incentives encourage meaningful progress. Metrics should illuminate the path, not replace it.

Historical and organizational examples demonstrate the consequences of prioritizing measurable targets over meaning. In the early 20th century, factory efficiency metrics emphasized speed and output, leading to unsafe working conditions and low-quality production. Modern corporations that track employee hours or tasks completed rather than quality or innovation often see similar outcomes. Public health initiatives that measure the number of vaccinations administered without tracking disease reduction may encourage quick but ineffective practices. In all cases, the behaviors that are rewarded reflect the metrics, not the underlying mission. Recognizing this pattern allows leaders to design measures that reinforce purpose rather than undermine it.

Even personal development is influenced by this principle. Individuals may track quantifiable achievements such as steps walked, books read, or dollars saved while neglecting the deeper purpose behind these actions. A person may achieve a high number of workouts per month but fail to improve strength, mobility, or long-term health because the focus was on the metric rather than meaningful progress. Similarly, tracking time spent on skill development without ensuring comprehension or mastery can create the illusion of growth. By aligning personal metrics with genuine outcomes—such as health improvements, mastery, or quality relationships—behavior becomes more meaningful and sustainable. The lesson is clear: metrics must serve meaning, not replace it.

In corporate innovation, metrics often distort intended outcomes. Research and development teams may be judged on the number of prototypes produced rather than breakthrough products or market success. Managers may prioritize reports, deadlines, or spreadsheet completion over customer satisfaction and long-term innovation. Employees respond to incentives embedded in these metrics, creating behavior that satisfies measurement rather than purpose. By designing metrics that track both activity and meaningful impact, organizations align behavior with intended outcomes. Leaders must regularly audit whether their metrics reinforce true objectives or encourage superficial compliance. Ensuring that measurement supports meaning transforms systems from a game of numbers into a path of real progress.

Financial systems illustrate the dangers of prioritizing metrics over substance. Investment portfolios often emphasize quarterly returns, stock price movement, or short-term ratios rather than long-term value creation. Traders respond to these metrics, sometimes taking excessive risk or manipulating appearances to hit targets. Similarly, government and corporate accounting systems may reward meeting numerical thresholds while ignoring sustainability, ethics, or quality. Redesigning incentives to focus on meaningful outcomes—such as long-term profitability, societal benefit, or stakeholder trust—changes behavior predictably. Metrics should guide decisions toward substantive success rather than serve as the sole measure of achievement. Meaningful measurement aligns immediate actions with long-term value.

Finally, overcoming the trap of metrics replacing meaning requires conscious system design. Leaders must distinguish between numbers that indicate progress and metrics that drive behavior. Rewards, recognition, and penalties should be tied to outcomes that reflect true purpose rather than superficial measures. Organizations, governments, and individuals should continuously reassess whether their metrics incentivize the behaviors they genuinely value. By ensuring that measurement reinforces mission, metrics become tools for alignment rather than sources of distortion. When meaning is prioritized over numbers, behavior naturally follows, producing sustainable and ethical results.

CHAPTER .8

GROWTH INCENTIVES ARE EATING THE WORLD

Relentless expansion incentives undermine environmental, social, and human stability.

The drive for growth dominates modern business, politics, and even personal ambition. Companies, governments, and individuals often prioritize expansion—more revenue, more followers, more output—without considering sustainability or long-term consequences. Incentives tied to growth reward short-term expansion while ignoring the environmental, social, and ethical costs. This relentless focus produces predictable distortions, such as resource depletion, inequality, and systemic fragility. Understanding how growth incentives shape behavior is essential for designing systems that balance expansion with stability. Leaders who fail to consider these dynamics risk creating unsustainable outcomes that ultimately undermine success.

In corporate environments, growth incentives are particularly powerful. Startups often prioritize user acquisition and revenue growth above profitability, operational stability, or employee well-being. Public companies focus on quarterly revenue and market share, sometimes sacrificing quality, ethics, or long-term strategy to satisfy investor expectations. These incentives encourage executives and employees to pursue growth at all costs, creating behaviors that harm brand reputation, sustainability, and morale. Companies that adjust incentives to reward customer satisfaction, operational efficiency, and long-term innovation align growth with sustainable success. Redesigning metrics and compensation structures ensures that expansion does not come at the expense of stability. Predictable behavior emerges when growth incentives are balanced with other priorities.

Government policies and economic systems also reflect the overemphasis on growth. GDP, population metrics, and short-term employment statistics often serve as primary indicators of success, encouraging leaders to pursue rapid expansion rather than long-term welfare. Policies may favor industrialization, resource extraction, or urban development without accounting for environmental impact, social cohesion, or future resilience. Citizens respond rationally to these incentives, often prioritizing immediate economic gains over sustainability. By redesigning policy incentives—such as rewarding renewable energy adoption, environmental conservation, or social equity—leaders can align behavior with long-term societal stability. Systems that over-prioritize growth create instability, while well-designed incentives promote sustainable prosperity.

Historical examples illustrate the destructive potential of unchecked growth incentives. Industrial expansion during the 19th and 20th centuries produced wealth but also severe pollution, labor exploitation, and resource depletion. Colonial powers expanded territories aggressively, prioritizing economic extraction over local welfare or ecological sustainability. These outcomes were not accidents; they were predictable results of incentive structures that rewarded growth above all else. Even modern corporations and governments repeat these patterns when short-term expansion is prioritized over sustainability. Understanding the underlying incentive structure allows leaders to design systems that reward growth responsibly, balancing ambition with long-term stewardship. Sustainable expansion requires careful attention to the incentives that drive behavior.

Even personal ambition can be distorted by growth-focused incentives. Individuals may pursue promotions, income, or social recognition relentlessly, neglecting health, relationships, or ethical considerations. The metrics for success—salary, title, social media following—become the target, rewarding expansion rather than meaningful achievement. By redefining personal incentives to value balance, well-being, and long-term contribution, individuals can pursue growth that is sustainable and fulfilling. Progress is naturally amplified when the rewards for behavior align with long-term goals rather than immediate visibility or accumulation. Recognizing the limits and costs of unchecked growth is essential for personal, organizational, and societal resilience.

Corporate strategies often suffer when growth incentives dominate decision-making. Businesses may prioritize market share or revenue above innovation, ethics, or employee well-being. Short-term revenue targets can encourage aggressive sales tactics, cost-cutting that harms quality, or layoffs that undermine morale. Companies that adjust incentives to reward customer satisfaction, employee development, and sustainable practices see healthier growth patterns. These adjustments create a self-reinforcing cycle where growth supports stability and innovation rather than undermining them. Leaders who understand the behavioral power of growth incentives can design systems that align expansion with ethical, environmental, and social responsibility. Sustainable growth is achieved by ensuring that what is rewarded produces long-term value rather than short-term volume.

Financial markets are also shaped by growth incentives. Investors often reward companies that deliver rapid returns, ignoring risk, ethical behavior, or long-term viability. Traders respond predictably, taking excessive risks to maximize short-term gains while ignoring systemic consequences. These incentives contributed to crises like the dot-com bubble and the 2008 financial meltdown, where growth at all costs created fragility. Regulatory frameworks that reward responsible investment, long-term performance, and risk management can counterbalance these pressures. Incentives, not ideology or morality, dictate behavior at scale in financial systems. Aligning growth incentives with sustainability is essential to prevent recurrent crises and ensure enduring prosperity.

Government and societal priorities are similarly influenced. Politicians and policymakers often emphasize economic growth, urban development, and industrial expansion while under-rewarding environmental stewardship, community cohesion, or social equity. Citizens and institutions respond to these signals, producing predictable patterns of behavior that prioritize immediate expansion. By creating incentives that reward ecological protection, social welfare, and long-term infrastructure resilience, governments can shift behavior toward sustainable outcomes. Balancing growth with stability requires intentional incentive design rather than reliance on moral appeals or voluntary compliance. Societies that fail to manage growth incentives risk environmental collapse, social unrest, and economic volatility.

Finally, overcoming the destructive power of growth incentives requires deliberate system design. Leaders must identify where expansion-focused rewards dominate and where they produce harmful consequences. Metrics, bonuses, regulations, and recognition should be structured to balance growth with sustainability, ethical behavior, and long-term impact. By aligning incentives with broader goals, leaders ensure that behaviors producing expansion also produce stability, well-being, and value. Individuals, organizations, and governments can achieve durable success when growth is incentivized responsibly. Understanding and redesigning growth incentives is essential for preserving resources, human capital, and societal resilience in the modern world.

CHAPTER .9

COMPETITION INCENTIVES OFTEN PUNISH COOPERATION

Many systems unintentionally reward selfish behavior while penalizing collaboration.

Competition is often celebrated as a driver of innovation, efficiency, and success, but when incentives are poorly designed, it can discourage cooperation and collective achievement. In many organizations and societies, rewards are tied to individual performance, rankings, or visibility, rather than team outcomes or shared success. This creates an environment where people prioritize personal gain over collective benefit, even when cooperation would produce better results. Collaboration, knowledge sharing, and mutual support are often undervalued or penalized, reducing overall system effectiveness. Understanding how competition-based incentives shape behavior is essential for designing systems that promote both individual excellence and collective success. Leaders must carefully balance competitive pressures with collaborative incentives to achieve sustainable outcomes.

In corporate environments, competition incentives often lead to counterproductive behavior. Sales teams rewarded solely on individual quotas may withhold leads, sabotage colleagues, or focus on short-term wins rather than long-term client satisfaction. Engineers and product teams may avoid sharing innovations if credit or recognition is granted only to the first contributor. Even high-performing employees can act selfishly when organizational rewards emphasize personal metrics over collective success. By redesigning incentives to reward team outcomes, knowledge sharing, and cross-functional collaboration, companies can create an environment where competition drives performance without undermining cooperation. Predictable behavior emerges when systems reward collaboration alongside individual achievement.

Government and policy systems illustrate similar patterns. Departments, agencies, and public officials often compete for budget, visibility, or political influence, even when collaboration would improve public outcomes. For instance, neighboring municipalities may withhold data or coordinate poorly because resources or recognition are allocated to the highest performer, not the most effective service. Public health initiatives can fail when organizations work in silos, prioritizing individual success metrics over collective impact. By aligning incentives to reward joint outcomes, shared metrics, and cooperative behavior, governments can encourage collaboration that produces superior results. Systems that over-emphasize competition inadvertently discourage cooperation, reducing societal effectiveness.

Historical and organizational examples demonstrate the risks of poorly designed competitive incentives. In the early 20th century, industrial firms competing for market dominance often cut corners on safety, labor standards, or environmental impact to outperform rivals. Academic institutions may emphasize publication counts over collaborative research or knowledge dissemination, reducing the overall impact of scholarship. Even social movements can fragment when recognition or funding is distributed to individuals or factions rather than the collective cause. These outcomes are not the result of moral failure but of rational responses to incentive structures. Understanding how competition shapes behavior allows leaders to design systems that reward both excellence and cooperation.

Even personal and team dynamics are affected by competitive incentives. In workplaces, families, and communities, individuals may hoard resources, information, or influence to outperform peers, sometimes undermining collective goals. Sports teams, academic groups, and professional projects all demonstrate that when only individual performance is rewarded, cooperation diminishes and outcomes suffer. Designing personal incentives—recognition, shared rewards, and collaborative goals—can encourage cooperative behavior alongside individual achievement. Teams respond predictably to the rewards embedded in their systems; when collaboration is incentivized, teamwork flourishes. Leaders, educators, and parents must balance competition with collaboration to ensure sustainable, high-performing systems.

In corporations, internal competition can undermine innovation. R&D teams may guard knowledge, duplicate efforts, or prioritize individual recognition over collective breakthrough solutions. Sales and marketing teams may compete destructively, reducing overall profitability and client satisfaction. Companies that implement team-based rewards, cross-functional bonuses, and collaborative recognition programs create environments where cooperation is rational and rewarding. Employees naturally adjust behavior to align with incentives, producing higher-quality outcomes, innovation, and morale. Competitive systems that fail to reward collaboration ultimately punish long-term performance despite short-term victories.

Financial and market competition also highlights the issue. Traders, firms, and investors may focus on beating rivals rather than creating value for clients or society. Short-term competition-based incentives encourage risk-taking, speculation, and aggressive tactics that can undermine systemic stability. Conversely, cooperative models, such as consortiums, partnerships, and shared research initiatives, can improve long-term outcomes if incentivized appropriately. Adjusting rewards to recognize both individual and collective success reduces destructive competition while maintaining high performance. The structure of incentives, not individual ambition, determines whether competition drives progress or conflict.

Government programs and international policy often suffer when competition dominates incentives. Countries, states, or agencies may withhold information, duplicate efforts, or prioritize political advantage over shared outcomes. Global challenges, such as climate change, pandemics, or cybersecurity, require cooperation, but competitive incentives often produce fragmented, ineffective responses. By redesigning incentive structures to reward collaboration, shared success, and transparent coordination, leaders can produce cooperative outcomes that surpass what individual effort alone could achieve. Systems that balance competition and cooperation are stronger, more resilient, and better aligned with long-term goals. Incentive architecture, not moral exhortation, shapes predictable behavior.

Finally, overcoming the destructive side of competition requires intentional design. Organizations, governments, and individuals must identify where rewards favor personal gain at the expense of collective achievement. By incorporating team-based metrics, joint recognition, and shared incentives, leaders can foster environments where collaboration and competition coexist productively. Predictable and sustainable behavior emerges when cooperation is rewarded alongside excellence. Recognizing that competition incentives often punish cooperation allows leaders to create balanced systems that amplify performance without undermining collective success. Designing incentives thoughtfully ensures that both individual and shared goals are consistently achieved.

Chapter .10

The Success Trap Keeps Broken Systems Alive

Systems that appear successful can still generate deeply harmful second-order effects.

Many systems survive not because they are effective, but because they appear successful in ways that satisfy immediate incentives. Organizations, governments, and institutions often measure performance through superficial metrics, reputations, or short-term gains rather than long-term impact. These perceived successes create a "success trap," where flawed systems continue to operate and expand because stakeholders are rewarded for appearances rather than results. Leaders and participants may resist change, believing the system works when the deeper consequences reveal dysfunction. Understanding the success trap is essential for diagnosing problems and redesigning incentives. True progress requires evaluating whether a system's apparent success aligns with meaningful, sustainable outcomes.

In corporate environments, the success trap is common. Companies may show strong revenue growth, market share, or stock performance while underlying processes, culture, or ethical practices deteriorate. Executives may be rewarded for short-term gains, while operational inefficiencies, employee disengagement, or environmental harm go unaddressed. Investors, employees, and regulators often focus on visible achievements, reinforcing the flawed system. By analyzing second-order effects and redesigning incentives to reward sustainability, ethical behavior, and long-term resilience, organizations can escape the success trap. Leadership must distinguish between apparent victories and actual progress to create lasting value. Misaligned incentives keep broken systems alive long after their utility has declined.

Government policies frequently fall into the success trap as well. Programs that show immediate outputs, like high enrollment numbers or rapid construction projects, may obscure inefficiencies, waste, or unintended social consequences. Policymakers receive praise for visible activity, even when the policies fail to achieve substantive impact over time. Bureaucracies reinforce these dynamics by rewarding compliance with metrics rather than outcomes. By redesigning incentives to reward real-world effectiveness, governments can correct systemic flaws and ensure that initiatives produce genuine results. Escaping the success trap requires evaluating deeper outcomes, not just visible indicators. Without this awareness, ineffective systems continue consuming resources and producing harm.

Historical examples illustrate the persistence of broken systems. Empires, corporations, and institutions often appear successful while sowing the seeds of their own decline. For instance, colonial administrations may have increased trade and revenue, creating the appearance of prosperity, while exploiting populations and resources in ways that undermined long-term stability. Similarly, industrial firms that focused on rapid output while ignoring environmental or labor consequences appeared successful but caused systemic harm. These examples reveal that apparent success can mask fundamental flaws, creating incentives to maintain the status quo. Recognizing the success trap allows leaders to intervene before long-term consequences undermine stability. True leadership requires looking beyond immediate signals of success to understand structural health.

Even personal habits and organizational cultures can be caught in the success trap. Individuals may maintain routines or behaviors that seem productive—working long hours, accumulating credentials, or achieving measurable milestones—while neglecting health, relationships, or meaningful goals. Teams may follow processes that appear efficient or compliant but generate long-term inefficiencies or ethical risks. By reassessing incentives and aligning rewards with substantive outcomes, people and organizations can escape patterns of superficial success. Small changes in incentive structure can shift behavior from maintaining appearances to producing meaningful results. Awareness of the success trap ensures that effort, recognition, and growth are directed toward outcomes that truly matter.

In business, the success trap can stifle innovation. Companies rewarded for maintaining existing markets or products may resist change, fearing disruption to current success metrics. Employees may avoid proposing bold ideas or experimentation, preserving the appearance of achievement while eroding long-term competitiveness. By redesigning incentives to reward innovation, learning from failure, and strategic risk-taking, organizations can overcome the trap and create sustainable growth. Recognition systems, performance evaluations, and compensation structures must reinforce desired long-term behaviors, not just current appearances. Predictable behavior emerges when incentives encourage substantive progress rather than superficial metrics. Escaping the success trap ensures systems evolve rather than stagnate under the illusion of effectiveness.

Financial systems illustrate the danger of perceived success. Companies may report strong quarterly earnings or high stock prices, masking excessive risk-taking, debt accumulation, or ethical compromises. Investors and regulators may celebrate these visible metrics without evaluating systemic stability, creating incentives for further risky behavior. Adjusting incentive structures to reward sustainable growth, risk management, and ethical governance mitigates the success trap. Financial and organizational health improves when the focus shifts from short-term appearance to long-term resilience. Leaders must anticipate the second-order effects of apparent success to prevent catastrophic failures. Escaping the success trap requires a deliberate focus on underlying system health, not just surface-level indicators.

Government and public institutions often maintain the status quo due to the success trap. Agencies may show high compliance rates, project completion, or political visibility while underlying inefficiencies, inequities, or long-term harm persist. Bureaucrats and elected officials are rewarded for maintaining these appearances, reinforcing behaviors that perpetuate systemic flaws. By redesigning metrics, incentives, and accountability mechanisms, leaders can encourage behaviors that generate real societal impact rather than superficial performance. Citizens, organizations, and governments respond predictably to these incentives, making the system self-reinforcing until deliberate intervention occurs. Recognizing the success trap is essential for sustainable policy design and public sector effectiveness.

Finally, escaping the success trap requires conscious leadership and incentive alignment. Leaders must distinguish between what appears successful and what produces meaningful, lasting outcomes. Systems should be evaluated for their long-term consequences, and incentives must reward behaviors that generate real value rather than superficial metrics. By identifying and correcting misalignments, organizations, governments, and individuals can transform seemingly effective systems into truly sustainable ones. Awareness of second-order effects allows leaders to break cycles that preserve dysfunction under the guise of achievement. The path to enduring success lies in rewarding outcomes that truly matter, not just appearances.

Part III — Incentives in Money, Markets, and Work

CHAPTER .11

PROFIT IS A TOOL, NOT A PURPOSE

Markets work best when profit incentives are aligned with real value creation.

Profit is often mistaken for the ultimate goal of business, but in reality, it is a tool for measuring and facilitating value creation. Organizations that treat profit as an end rather than a means risk prioritizing short-term gain over sustainable growth, ethical behavior, and customer satisfaction. When profit becomes the sole purpose, employees and leaders may focus on maximizing revenue at the expense of quality, innovation, or social responsibility. Viewing profit as a tool allows businesses to align financial incentives with creating genuine value for customers, society, and stakeholders. Understanding the role of profit within a broader system of incentives is essential for sustainable success. Leaders who treat profit as a means rather than an end can build organizations that thrive ethically and economically.

Corporate examples illustrate the importance of viewing profit as a tool. Companies that prioritize profit above all else may engage in practices like cost-cutting, misleading marketing, or overworking employees to boost short-term earnings. These strategies can generate impressive financial results temporarily but often damage brand reputation, employee morale, and long-term competitiveness. Conversely, organizations that view profit as a reward for creating real value focus on customer satisfaction, innovation, and employee development. Aligning profit with meaningful outcomes incentivizes behaviors that support sustainability, quality, and ethical practices. By reframing profit as a tool, companies can balance financial success with long-term stability and social responsibility. The way profit is incentivized determines the actions that employees and leaders take.

In government and public policy, the concept of profit as a tool translates to resource allocation and efficiency. Agencies and institutions often measure success by budgets spent, revenue collected, or outputs produced rather than the real value delivered to citizens. For instance, a public-private partnership may focus on maximizing financial returns while neglecting service quality or public welfare. By treating profit as a mechanism for enabling positive outcomes rather than an end, policymakers can structure incentives that reward both efficiency and impact. Governments can encourage socially responsible business practices through taxation, subsidies, or regulatory incentives that align profit with meaningful societal outcomes. Aligning financial incentives with public value ensures markets work for the long-term benefit of all stakeholders.

Historical examples demonstrate the risks of treating profit as an end in itself. Industrialization in the 19th century created enormous wealth, yet many companies exploited labor, degraded the environment, and neglected community welfare in the pursuit of maximum profit. These strategies provided short-term financial success but left long-term social and ecological consequences. In contrast, businesses that reinvested profits into employee development, community engagement, and sustainable practices generated enduring growth and stability. The principle is clear: profit is most effective when it rewards value creation rather than appearing as the sole objective. Leaders who understand this distinction can design incentive systems that encourage productive, ethical, and sustainable behavior.

Even personal and entrepreneurial decisions are influenced by the understanding of profit as a tool. Individuals may pursue income and financial gain without considering the broader consequences of their actions, creating stress, ethical compromise, or societal harm. Entrepreneurs who view profit as a mechanism to fund innovation, growth, and positive impact tend to make decisions that benefit both themselves and the communities they serve. By aligning personal financial incentives with meaningful contributions, individuals can achieve sustainable success and fulfillment. Profit becomes a signal of value creation rather than a justification for harmful behavior. Designing personal systems around profit as a tool ensures decisions are both ethical and effective.

Financial systems illustrate the importance of this principle. Investors and companies that focus solely on maximizing short-term returns often take excessive risks, neglect long-term growth, or engage in unethical behavior. By incentivizing long-term value creation, risk management, and ethical practices, markets can channel profit toward productive, sustainable outcomes. Financial incentives that reward innovation, customer satisfaction, and responsible governance encourage behavior that benefits all stakeholders. When profit functions as a tool, it provides feedback about the effectiveness of value creation rather than dictating behavior. Leaders and market participants who understand this distinction can make decisions that are profitable, ethical, and sustainable simultaneously.

Corporate culture is heavily influenced by how profit is framed within the organization. If compensation, promotion, and recognition systems emphasize revenue without context, employees will optimize for financial outcomes, often at the expense of innovation, quality, or collaboration. By integrating profit with broader metrics like customer impact, employee engagement, and social responsibility, companies create an environment where financial success is a natural outcome of value creation. Leaders who design incentive systems with this understanding cultivate behaviors that align profitability with purpose. Profit becomes a reinforcing tool, not a dominating objective. Organizations that internalize this principle consistently outperform those that chase profit as an isolated goal.

Finally, mastering profit as a tool requires deliberate design and mindset. Leaders, entrepreneurs, and policymakers must distinguish between profit as a signal of value and profit as a goal in itself. Incentives should reward behaviors that create genuine value for customers, employees, and society, with profit emerging naturally as a result. Systems that prioritize profit without context encourage short-termism, unethical behavior, and unsustainable practices. By embedding profit within a framework of meaningful outcomes, leaders create organizations, policies, and personal strategies that thrive ethically and economically. Understanding profit as a tool, not a purpose, transforms markets and institutions into engines of sustainable, responsible growth.

CHAPTER .12

EXECUTIVE INCENTIVES EXPLAIN CORPORATE FAILURE

Short-term compensation structures encourage risk-taking that endangers entire organizations.

Executive behavior is heavily shaped by the incentives built into their compensation, promotion, and recognition structures. When rewards prioritize short-term financial performance, executives are motivated to make decisions that boost immediate metrics, even at the expense of long-term organizational health. Stock options, bonuses, and quarterly targets often encourage excessive risk, cost-cutting, or unethical practices that can jeopardize the company. These behaviors are rational responses to the incentive system, not evidence of moral failure or incompetence. Understanding executive incentives is crucial to explaining why corporations fail despite having talented leaders. Aligning executive rewards with sustainable, long-term outcomes ensures decisions benefit the entire organization and its stakeholders.

Corporate failures often illustrate the destructive power of misaligned executive incentives. The 2008 financial crisis provides a stark example: executives pursued high-risk lending, securitization, and speculative investments to maximize short-term bonuses while ignoring long-term exposure and systemic risk. Similarly, companies that emphasize stock price growth over operational health may underinvest in infrastructure, R&D, or workforce development, creating fragility. Executives respond predictably to incentives embedded in compensation, highlighting that the design of these structures determines behavior. By redesigning incentives to reward long-term value creation, risk management, and ethical conduct, organizations can prevent the behaviors that lead to failure. Incentive architecture, not moral exhortation, drives executive decisions.

Board governance and oversight play a critical role in shaping executive incentives. Boards that link CEO and executive compensation to quarterly performance metrics often unintentionally encourage short-termism. Conversely, boards that tie rewards to multi-year growth, sustainability metrics, innovation, and employee engagement foster long-term strategic thinking. When executive incentives align with broader organizational goals, leaders make decisions that balance immediate performance with enduring stability. Companies that fail to design effective governance and incentive structures expose themselves to predictable risks, including financial collapse, reputational damage, and loss of talent. Understanding how executive rewards shape behavior allows boards to steer corporations toward sustainable success.

Historical and contemporary corporate examples demonstrate this principle repeatedly. Enron, Lehman Brothers, and WorldCom all collapsed partly due to executive incentive structures that rewarded short-term stock performance and financial engineering over transparency and ethical governance. Conversely, organizations that link executive compensation to customer satisfaction, innovation, and long-term profitability often outperform peers in resilience and market value. These cases show that executive behavior is a rational response to incentives rather than an aberration. Redesigning executive rewards can prevent catastrophic organizational failures and align leaders' behavior with the long-term health of the company. Incentive alignment is a predictive tool for organizational stability and success.

Even in smaller organizations and startups, executive incentives influence decision-making profoundly. Founders and early executives often prioritize rapid growth or visibility to attract investors, sometimes neglecting operational soundness, ethics, or employee well-being. Incentive structures that reward sustainable growth, product quality, and team development encourage leaders to make decisions that benefit both the company and stakeholders. Startups that align executive incentives with long-term mission and customer value avoid the pitfalls of rapid but unstable expansion. Predictable outcomes emerge when leaders' rewards reflect organizational priorities rather than individual short-term gain. Incentive design is therefore central to guiding executive behavior in organizations of all sizes.

Financial institutions highlight the consequences of misaligned executive incentives. Traders and investment managers often focus on strategies that maximize short-term bonuses while externalizing long-term risk to the organization or market. Banks and investment firms that link executive compensation to long-term performance, risk-adjusted returns, and compliance reduce reckless behavior. Incentives shape behavior at the executive level in ways that have system-wide consequences, demonstrating the importance of thoughtful design. Aligning incentives with sustainable outcomes transforms risky short-term decisions into strategic long-term growth. The structure of executive rewards explains why companies thrive or fail.

Government and regulatory frameworks also interact with executive incentives. Weak oversight or poorly designed reporting requirements allow executives to exploit incentive structures for personal gain, sometimes at the expense of employees, shareholders, or the public. Strong regulations that require transparency, long-term accountability, and ethical governance counteract perverse incentives and align executive behavior with societal interests. Incentive design at the executive level interacts with broader systemic rules to shape corporate outcomes. Leaders, boards, and policymakers must work together to create structures where rational responses to rewards benefit the organization and society. Understanding executive incentives explains failure and enables solutions that prevent recurrence.

Finally, mastering executive incentive design requires a comprehensive understanding of human behavior and organizational systems. Rewards, penalties, recognition, and accountability mechanisms must be structured to encourage decisions that produce sustainable, ethical, and strategic outcomes. Misaligned incentives predictably drive behaviors that increase risk, harm stakeholders, and undermine long-term value. By aligning executive incentives with organizational mission, customer value, employee engagement, and ethical standards, leaders can transform high-risk decision-making into sustainable growth. Incentive design is the bridge between executive action and corporate health, making it a central tool for preventing organizational failure. Systems succeed or fail based on how leaders are incentivized to act.

Chapter .13

Why Workers Disengage When Incentives Ignore Humanity

Productivity declines when incentives treat people as replaceable inputs.

Organizations often design incentives focused solely on output, efficiency, or measurable performance, neglecting the human needs of employees. When people feel undervalued, overworked, or disconnected from purpose, engagement and productivity naturally decline. Incentives that ignore humanity—such as purely quantitative targets, rigid schedules, or one-size-fits-all rewards—treat workers as replaceable parts rather than creative, motivated individuals. Conversely, systems that recognize contributions, foster growth, and support well-being encourage engagement, innovation, and loyalty. Understanding the human dimension of incentives is critical for creating productive and sustainable workplaces. Leaders who fail to consider this risk driving disengagement and high turnover.

Corporate examples illustrate this dynamic clearly. Companies that reward only sales volume, production numbers, or hours worked often experience disengaged employees, absenteeism, and burnout. Staff may comply superficially to achieve metrics, but creativity, collaboration, and discretionary effort decline. In contrast, organizations that integrate recognition, autonomy, and professional development into incentive structures see higher engagement and better outcomes. Employees respond predictably to systems that respect their humanity, aligning effort with meaningful contribution. Engagement is not just a matter of motivation—it is a direct response to how incentives are designed. Treating employees as people rather than inputs produces both ethical and practical benefits.

Even small adjustments in incentive structures can profoundly affect worker engagement. Providing flexible schedules, career growth opportunities, and recognition programs addresses human needs while still promoting organizational goals. Performance metrics that consider collaboration, customer satisfaction, and problem-solving encourage employees to contribute in ways that align with both mission and personal fulfillment. By valuing intrinsic as well as extrinsic motivators, organizations tap into deeper sources of productivity. Workers are more willing to invest discretionary effort when incentives acknowledge their contributions beyond raw output. Leaders who design human-centered incentives create a culture of engagement and innovation.

Government and public institutions face similar challenges. Employees in bureaucracies often encounter rigid procedures, compliance-focused rewards, and limited recognition for initiative. These systems reduce intrinsic motivation and discourage creative problem-solving. Policymakers and public managers who redesign incentives to reward problem-solving, collaboration, and citizen impact can dramatically improve engagement and efficiency. Employees respond predictably to incentives, adjusting behavior based on what is recognized and rewarded. Human-centered incentive design increases organizational effectiveness while also improving employee satisfaction. Recognizing and addressing the human element in work is essential for functional institutions.

Historical examples highlight the consequences of ignoring humanity in incentive design. Factories during the industrial revolution prioritized output above worker safety, satisfaction, or personal development. High turnover, low morale, and resistance were predictable results of these incentive structures. Modern organizations that focus solely on productivity metrics risk repeating these patterns on a subtler scale. Conversely, firms that reward collaboration, creativity, and well-being see sustainable performance and loyalty. Systems that treat humans as replaceable components may succeed temporarily, but long-term engagement and success require recognizing human needs. Leaders who integrate human-centered incentives create workplaces that are both productive and humane.

Financial systems and corporate hierarchies further illustrate this principle. When compensation, promotions, or recognition emphasize short-term financial results over teamwork, ethical behavior, or personal growth, employees may disengage or act opportunistically. Conversely, aligning incentives with sustainable performance, skill development, and ethical behavior encourages engagement and accountability. Companies that embed humanity into their incentive structures reduce turnover, increase innovation, and improve morale. Incentives, when thoughtfully designed, create predictable patterns of behavior, guiding employees toward productive and meaningful contributions. Recognizing the human dimension ensures that work systems are both effective and sustainable.

Even in small teams and personal projects, ignoring humanity has consequences. Volunteers, collaborators, and freelancers respond to incentives that recognize their effort, provide autonomy, and reinforce meaningful outcomes. Systems that focus exclusively on output without consideration of human needs produce disengagement, reduced creativity, and inconsistent performance. By embedding recognition, growth opportunities, and personal accountability into incentives, leaders cultivate motivated and productive contributors. Engagement becomes a natural response when incentives respect individual humanity and dignity. Leaders who understand this principle design systems that harness human potential rather than suppress it.

Finally, mastering human-centered incentive design requires conscious attention to both tangible and intangible motivators. Recognition, autonomy, career growth, meaningful work, and fair treatment are as important as financial rewards. Organizations, governments, and individuals must balance measurable outputs with support for intrinsic motivation. Predictable and sustainable engagement emerges when human needs are embedded in incentives alongside organizational goals. Leaders who ignore humanity risk disengagement, reduced productivity, and ethical lapses. Aligning incentives with human needs ensures that work is meaningful, sustainable, and productive, producing both organizational and personal benefits.

Chapter .14

Innovation Thrives When Failure Is Properly Incentivized

Creative progress requires systems that reward intelligent risk rather than punish it.

Innovation is inherently risky, and systems that penalize failure often stifle creativity and experimentation. When individuals or organizations fear negative consequences for trying new approaches, they naturally prioritize safety over exploration. Conversely, properly structured incentives that tolerate intelligent failure encourage experimentation, learning, and breakthroughs. Organizations, governments, and individuals that align rewards with thoughtful risk-taking produce more innovative and adaptive outcomes. Understanding how to incentivize failure responsibly is essential for cultivating sustainable innovation. Leaders who ignore this dynamic inadvertently discourage the very behaviors that drive progress.

Corporate examples highlight the power of failure-positive incentives. Tech companies like Google and Amazon allocate resources to experimental projects and encourage employees to pursue bold ideas, knowing that not all will succeed. Teams are rewarded for learning from mistakes and iterating, rather than penalized for missing short-term targets. In contrast, organizations that punish failure with demotions, public criticism, or job insecurity drive employees toward predictable, low-risk behavior.

Properly designed incentives encourage experimentation that aligns with organizational objectives, producing both innovation and resilience. Companies that reward intelligent risk-taking are more likely to develop breakthrough products and services. Predictable, long-term success emerges when failure is treated as a valuable learning opportunity.

Government programs and public policies benefit from similar approaches. Agencies that encourage experimentation in social programs, infrastructure projects, or research initiatives achieve higher rates of innovation. For instance, pilot programs with flexible evaluation frameworks allow governments to test new approaches without fear of punitive consequences for temporary setbacks. By incentivizing learning from failure, policymakers foster systems that adapt, improve, and scale effective solutions. Punishing failure, on the other hand, encourages risk-avoidance, inefficiency, and stagnation. Aligning incentives to reward experimentation ensures that public initiatives evolve based on evidence and real-world outcomes. Innovation in public systems requires an environment where failure is both safe and informative.

Historical examples demonstrate how failure-positive cultures foster innovation. The Wright brothers' repeated unsuccessful flights taught lessons that ultimately enabled the first successful airplane. Thomas Edison's thousands of unsuccessful experiments with the lightbulb were steps toward a transformative invention. In contrast, organizations or societies that punish failure often suppress experimentation, losing opportunities for progress. Properly incentivizing failure recognizes its role as a necessary component of discovery and adaptation. Leaders who cultivate a culture where mistakes are analyzed rather than punished accelerate the pace of meaningful innovation. Systems that embrace failure intelligently produce adaptive, resilient, and creative solutions.

Even personal growth and entrepreneurship are shaped by failure incentives. Individuals who fear mistakes may avoid pursuing ambitious goals, learning opportunities, or skill development. Entrepreneurs often succeed because they are willing to take calculated risks, iterate, and learn from setbacks. Rewarding persistence, reflection, and iterative improvement creates behavior that aligns with long-term success. Personal incentive systems—such as habit tracking, mentorship feedback, and milestone recognition—can reinforce learning from failure. When failure is properly incentivized, individuals are more willing to experiment, adapt, and grow. Understanding and embracing intelligent failure is a key driver of personal and professional development.

Corporate structures often determine whether failure leads to innovation or stagnation. Rigid hierarchies, inflexible metrics, and punitive review systems discourage risk-taking and slow progress. Companies that integrate cross-functional collaboration, rapid prototyping, and safe-to-fail experiments encourage behaviors that generate insights and breakthroughs. Leaders who reward initiative, learning, and resilience create teams that approach challenges creatively rather than defensively. Incentives determine whether employees perceive failure as a threat or a tool for improvement. Properly designed systems produce predictable patterns of innovation and adaptation across organizations.

Financial and venture ecosystems also rely on intelligent risk-taking. Investors and startup incubators understand that failure is a natural part of high-potential innovation. Funding mechanisms that reward learning from mistakes, pivoting, and experimentation accelerate the development of transformative ideas. Conversely, environments that punish failure or focus solely on immediate returns discourage risk-taking and slow progress. Incentive structures shape behavior predictably: when intelligent failure is rewarded, innovation thrives. Leaders and investors alike must design reward systems that tolerate setbacks while fostering learning.

Government, academia, and research institutions illustrate the same principle. Policies that fund experiments, support pilot studies, and provide flexible evaluation criteria encourage scientists and innovators to explore bold solutions. Conversely, rigid bureaucracies that punish negative results stifle creativity and prevent adaptation. Properly aligned incentives reward learning, risk management, and evidence-based iteration, fostering more effective research and public programs. Systems that tolerate failure while rewarding reflection produce better long-term outcomes than those that demand infallibility. Innovation requires a culture that understands failure as a necessary part of growth, not a liability.

Finally, mastering failure-positive incentives requires conscious design and cultural reinforcement. Leaders must distinguish between careless mistakes and intelligent risk-taking, rewarding behaviors that promote learning and adaptation. Organizations, governments, and individuals benefit when setbacks are analyzed, shared, and integrated into future planning. By embedding these principles into incentive structures, failure becomes a stepping stone rather than a barrier to progress. Predictable innovation emerges when systems reward experimentation and learning, not just success. Properly incentivized failure transforms risk into an engine for growth, creativity, and long-term achievement.

Chapter .15

The Future of Work Depends on Incentive Redesign

Sustainable productivity emerges when incentives align personal growth with organizational success.

The nature of work is changing rapidly due to technology, globalization, and shifting societal expectations. Traditional incentive structures—fixed salaries, rigid hierarchies, and narrow performance metrics—are increasingly misaligned with the demands of modern work. Employees seek purpose, autonomy, and growth, while organizations need innovation, adaptability, and collaboration. Redesigning incentives to align individual motivation with organizational goals ensures sustainable productivity and engagement. Systems that fail to adapt risk disengagement, turnover, and inefficiency. Understanding how incentives shape behavior is essential for preparing the workforce of the future.

Corporate environments provide clear examples of the need for incentive redesign. Companies that continue to reward hours worked or output alone struggle to retain talent and foster creativity. In contrast, organizations that incorporate flexible schedules, performance-based recognition, skill development opportunities, and cross-functional collaboration see higher engagement and innovation. Employees respond predictably to rewards that match their intrinsic and extrinsic motivations. Incentives that emphasize learning, growth, and meaningful contribution align individual behavior with organizational success. By focusing on the human dimension of work, companies create sustainable performance and long-term competitiveness.

Government and policy institutions face similar challenges in adapting work incentives. Public sector employees often operate under rigid rules, performance evaluations based solely on compliance, and minimal recognition for innovation. These structures discourage proactive problem-solving and creativity, reducing organizational effectiveness. Redesigning public sector incentives to reward collaboration, initiative, and impact can improve service delivery and employee satisfaction. Policymakers must recognize that modern work demands a balance between accountability and empowerment. Aligning incentives with meaningful outcomes ensures that employees contribute effectively to public goals while developing their own skills and capabilities.

Historical examples demonstrate the consequences of outdated incentive structures. Industrial-era factories rewarded repetitive labor and adherence to strict routines, producing efficiency but suppressing creativity and engagement. Modern organizations that maintain similar approaches risk the same outcomes: low morale, stagnation, and high turnover. Conversely, organizations that redesign incentives to reward skill development, adaptability, and purpose-driven work cultivate innovation and resilience. The link between incentive design and long-term organizational performance is clear: systems that evolve with changing work demands succeed, while rigid structures fail. Predictable behavior emerges when rewards are aligned with meaningful and sustainable goals.

Personal and professional development is deeply influenced by work incentives. Individuals who are rewarded solely for output or metrics may experience burnout, disengagement, or skill stagnation. Conversely, incentives that promote mastery, autonomy, collaboration, and growth motivate individuals to invest in meaningful work. Mentorship programs, project-based recognition, and opportunities for skill acquisition align personal development with organizational objectives. By creating feedback loops that reward learning and impact, employees engage more deeply with their work. Redesigning incentives at both organizational and personal levels ensures that productivity, satisfaction, and innovation are mutually reinforced.

Corporate culture is shaped by how work incentives are structured. Traditional hierarchies and rigid performance metrics often discourage experimentation, collaboration, and accountability. In contrast, flexible systems that reward initiative, cross-team cooperation, and innovative problem-solving foster a culture of adaptability. Employees naturally adjust behavior to match the rewards provided, producing better outcomes when incentives encourage the behaviors the organization values. Aligning rewards with both organizational objectives and individual growth creates a self-reinforcing cycle of engagement, innovation, and resilience. Incentive redesign is therefore central to creating the future-ready workplace.

Financial systems and performance metrics also influence work behavior. Companies that link bonuses and evaluations to short-term results may encourage risk-taking, corner-cutting, or overemphasis on easily measurable outputs. Redesigning incentive structures to reward long-term value creation, ethical behavior, and skill development mitigates these risks. Employees respond predictably to reward systems, making it possible to guide behavior toward sustainable outcomes. Properly designed financial and recognition incentives align personal effort with organizational success. The future of work depends on embedding thoughtful incentive structures across all levels of the organization.

Government, public policy, and societal structures are also adapting to changes in work incentives. Programs that encourage lifelong learning, professional development, and cross-sector collaboration reward behaviors aligned with modern workforce needs. Conversely, rigid evaluation systems focused on compliance or standardized outputs fail to foster innovation and adaptability. By aligning incentives with skill acquisition, collaboration, and societal impact, governments can support a workforce prepared for the evolving demands of the 21st century. Incentives shape behavior predictably, creating either adaptive or stagnant systems. Redesigning incentives ensures that individuals and organizations thrive in a rapidly changing environment.

Finally, mastering work incentive redesign requires a holistic approach. Leaders must consider intrinsic motivators, such as purpose, autonomy, and mastery, alongside extrinsic rewards like compensation, recognition, and career advancement. Systems that balance personal growth with organizational objectives produce sustainable engagement, innovation, and performance. Individuals and organizations naturally adjust behavior to align with incentives, making thoughtful design essential for long-term success. The future of work depends not on technology alone, but on aligning human motivation with systemic incentives. By redesigning incentives, leaders ensure that work is productive, meaningful, and resilient in an era of rapid change.

Part IV — Incentives in Government, Policy, and Power

Chapter .16

Politicians Respond to Incentives, Not Promises

Electoral systems shape political behavior more than rhetoric or ideology.

Political behavior is rarely determined solely by ideology or personal convictions; incentives embedded within electoral, legislative, and party systems largely guide decision-making. Politicians respond predictably to the structures that reward votes, campaign contributions, media attention, or reelection prospects. Promises, moral appeals, and policy ideals often take a backseat to these tangible incentives, shaping behavior in ways that may not align with long-term societal benefit. Understanding these incentives is critical for citizens, policymakers, and reformers who seek meaningful change. Systems, not individual character, often determine political action. Redesigning incentives in governance is therefore essential to encourage decisions that serve public interest rather than short-term advantage.

Electoral systems provide a clear example of incentive-driven behavior. Politicians seeking reelection respond to incentives such as campaign donations, media exposure, and voter attention, sometimes prioritizing popular measures over effective policy. Policies that require long-term investment, structural reform, or unpopular decisions may be ignored because immediate electoral rewards are absent. Conversely, systems that reward accountability, transparency, and long-term results encourage politicians to make choices aligned with sustainable public welfare. Understanding the incentives embedded in electoral processes reveals why many governments emphasize visibility and rhetoric over substantive progress. Citizens and reformers must analyze incentives to predict and influence political behavior effectively.

Government bureaucracy and institutional structures also shape political incentives. Legislators and administrators often prioritize initiatives that expand budgets, increase visibility, or generate short-term wins rather than addressing systemic problems. Programs that require long-term planning or cross-agency coordination may be avoided because the political payoff is delayed or uncertain. By designing incentives that reward cooperation, measurable societal improvement, and long-term stewardship, governments can redirect political behavior toward meaningful outcomes. Leaders act predictably within systems, responding to incentives rather than abstract ideals. Effective policy reform requires restructuring these systems to align incentives with public interest rather than personal or political gain.

Historical examples illustrate how incentives dominate political action. Leaders in various eras and regions often pursued policies that strengthened their political standing rather than the long-term welfare of citizens. Decisions regarding taxation, war, public spending, and social reform were frequently influenced by the incentives of survival, popularity, or control rather than moral or ideological principles. Even well-intentioned leaders are constrained by the incentive structures of their time. Recognizing this dynamic allows reformers to focus on altering the system rather than expecting individual virtue to drive change. Incentive alignment in politics is therefore the most reliable predictor of policy outcomes.

Even at a personal and local level, political behavior reflects incentive structures. Community leaders, school boards, or municipal councils respond to recognition, funding, and public approval more than abstract commitments to ethical ideals. Incentive-aware governance ensures that these actors prioritize actions that produce measurable benefits, engage constituents, and foster sustainable community outcomes. By designing reward systems—such as accountability metrics, public performance evaluations, and transparent reporting—leaders can guide behavior toward collective good. Predictable responses to incentives make it possible to shape politics through structural design rather than relying solely on moral persuasion. Understanding the primacy of incentives in political behavior empowers citizens and policymakers alike.

Corporate and lobbying interactions further illustrate the influence of incentives on political decisions. Legislators often respond to financial contributions, lobbying pressure, and regulatory influence rather than the merits of policies themselves. Companies and advocacy groups exploit these predictable behaviors by structuring influence to align with political incentives. Reforms that increase transparency, reduce conflicts of interest, and reward ethical decision-making can realign incentives toward public benefit. Politicians adjust behavior to match the rewards and consequences they perceive. Aligning political incentives with societal good ensures that elected officials act predictably in favor of the public rather than narrow interests.

Media and public opinion also shape political incentives. Politicians are rewarded for attention-grabbing actions, soundbites, and visibility, sometimes at the expense of substantive problem-solving. Social media, polling, and coverage metrics create incentives that prioritize short-term popularity over long-term policy effectiveness. Designing accountability mechanisms, performance metrics, and public engagement strategies that reward thoughtful decision-making counteracts these tendencies. Incentives guide behavior predictably, whether in corporations, communities, or national governments. Reforming political systems to focus rewards on meaningful outcomes aligns politicians' actions with long-term public interest.

Finally, mastering the influence of incentives in politics requires structural thinking. Citizens, policymakers, and institutions must recognize that rhetoric and promises are insufficient to predict behavior. Electoral rules, funding mechanisms, media attention, and institutional rewards shape choices far more than idealistic statements. By realigning these incentives to reward outcomes that benefit the public—transparency, effectiveness, and long-term planning—societies can produce predictable and positive political behavior. Leaders respond to the system they operate in, and changing the system changes the behavior. Incentive redesign in politics is therefore the most reliable pathway to effective governance.

Chapter .17

Policy Failure Is Usually an Incentive Failure

Regulations backfire when compliance incentives outweigh outcome incentives.

Policies and regulations often fail not because the objectives are misguided, but because the incentives embedded within them encourage the wrong behavior. Organizations, bureaucrats, and citizens respond predictably to the rewards and penalties they face, which may differ from the policy's intended outcomes. Compliance-focused incentives, where meeting procedural requirements is rewarded over achieving actual results, can produce superficial success while real-world problems persist. Understanding that incentives drive behavior is essential for designing policies that succeed. When systems prioritize compliance metrics over meaningful impact, policies fail despite best intentions. Redesigning incentives ensures that desired outcomes are both measurable and achievable.

Corporate and regulatory examples illustrate this dynamic. Environmental regulations that reward paperwork completion rather than actual emissions reduction can result in organizations meeting the letter of the law while continuing harmful practices. Financial regulations that emphasize reporting rather than risk management encourage firms to game metrics instead of reducing systemic risk. Employees and executives respond rationally to the incentives they face, focusing on what is rewarded rather than what is meaningful. Policies that fail to account for human behavior and incentive structures are doomed to underperform. By aligning rewards with desired outcomes, organizations can achieve compliance that also produces tangible impact. Proper incentive design is the cornerstone of effective policy implementation.

Government programs often suffer from incentive misalignment. Social welfare initiatives may reward enrollment numbers rather than long-term quality of life improvements for recipients. Educational policies that reward standardized test performance rather than mastery encourage teaching to the test and discourage holistic learning. Policymakers must recognize that participants, administrators, and institutions respond to incentives embedded within the system. Aligning rewards with actual impact—such as improved health outcomes, skill mastery, or social equity—produces predictable, positive results. Failure to address incentives perpetuates inefficiency, corruption, and wasted resources. Understanding the behavioral dimension of policy is key to achieving meaningful societal change.

Historical examples reveal the perils of ignoring incentive structures in policy. Prohibition in the United States was intended to reduce alcohol consumption but inadvertently created black markets, organized crime, and unsafe production because the legal incentives promoted circumvention rather than compliance. Rent control policies, while aiming to protect tenants, sometimes encouraged landlords to reduce maintenance or convert properties to avoid constraints. These failures were not the result of bad intentions, but of misaligned incentives that drove predictable behaviors counter to the policy goals. By examining second-order effects and behavioral responses, policymakers can anticipate unintended consequences. Properly designed incentive structures prevent policy from backfiring and maximize effectiveness.

Even personal and organizational policies are shaped by incentive design. Workplace rules, performance metrics, and reward systems can unintentionally encourage minimal effort, rule circumvention, or short-term focus. Personal development plans that reward hours logged rather than skill acquisition, for example, incentivize busywork over meaningful growth. By designing policies that reward real outcomes—such as mastery, collaboration, or long-term contribution—individuals and organizations produce predictable and positive behaviors. Incentive-aware policy design ensures alignment between effort, reward, and desired results. Recognizing that policy failure is often a failure of incentives allows leaders to craft systems that reliably achieve intended objectives.

Corporate innovation is similarly influenced by policy incentives. Incentives that reward product launches over quality, profitability, or long-term adoption can result in wasted resources and diminished brand value. Employees focus on what is measured and rewarded, not on what is strategically important. Conversely, incentive structures that reward impact, learning, and sustainable success guide behavior toward outcomes that benefit both the company and its customers. Metrics, bonuses, and recognition must align with organizational objectives to prevent predictable misalignment. Policy, whether internal or external, is effective only when the incentives it creates drive the desired behavior. Aligning these incentives transforms potential failure into sustainable success.

Financial systems demonstrate the same principle. Accounting regulations, tax codes, and reporting requirements can encourage behavior that meets formal rules while undermining broader economic stability. Firms respond predictably to incentives by maximizing reported earnings, minimizing tax liability, or manipulating compliance metrics. Designing incentive-aligned policies that reward sustainable financial practices, transparency, and risk management reduces the likelihood of systemic failures. Investors, employees, and regulators adjust behavior in response to these signals, making incentive-aware design essential. When incentives focus on true outcomes rather than formal compliance, policy succeeds where it might otherwise fail. Understanding this dynamic is critical for long-term economic health.

Public sector and government programs often face similar challenges. Agencies may prioritize metrics like project completion or budget usage over actual social or economic impact, resulting in wasted resources and diminished trust. Citizens, administrators, and stakeholders respond predictably to these incentives, producing superficial success without real improvement. Designing policies that reward measurable impact, accountability, and innovation aligns behavior with societal objectives. Incentive-aware public administration ensures that resources are used effectively and programs achieve intended outcomes. Recognizing that policy failure is frequently a consequence of incentive misalignment is essential for creating functioning, adaptive systems.

Finally, mastering policy design requires a deep understanding of human behavior and incentive structures. Policies must reward the right actions and discourage behaviors that undermine objectives. Misaligned incentives produce predictable failures, while well-aligned systems guide organizations, governments, and individuals toward desired outcomes. Leaders must evaluate not only the stated goals of a policy but also how incentives shape decision-making and behavior. By prioritizing outcome-aligned incentives, policymakers can design systems that succeed predictably and sustainably. Understanding that policy failure is usually an incentive failure is the first step toward crafting effective, impactful rules.

CHAPTER .18

BUREAUCRACIES OPTIMIZE FOR SURVIVAL, NOT SERVICE

Institutional incentives prioritize self-preservation over public benefit.

Bureaucracies are designed to administer systems, policies, and organizations, but the incentives they face often prioritize survival, growth, and reputation over actual service. Departments, agencies, and teams respond predictably to the rewards and penalties embedded in their structures, focusing on maintaining budgets, staff, and authority rather than achieving outcomes. Rules, procedures, and reporting requirements are often optimized to protect the institution rather than to serve citizens or stakeholders. Understanding this survival instinct is crucial for policymakers, leaders, and reformers seeking meaningful change. Systems that reward self-preservation over effectiveness produce predictable inefficiencies and dysfunction. Redesigning incentives is essential to align bureaucratic behavior with intended societal or organizational goals.

Corporate analogues illustrate similar dynamics. Departments that prioritize internal metrics, risk avoidance, or visibility often optimize processes that protect the team or division rather than benefit the organization or customers. For instance, compliance teams may focus on paperwork and audits rather than identifying and addressing systemic risks. Employees respond predictably to the structures in which they operate, prioritizing actions that protect their position and resources. Organizations that redesign internal incentives to reward outcomes, collaboration, and customer satisfaction foster behavior that aligns with broader objectives. Institutional survival is natural, but without incentive alignment, it undermines mission effectiveness. Leaders must recognize the tension between internal preservation and external impact.

Government bureaucracies also demonstrate the survival instinct in policy execution. Agencies frequently prioritize protecting their budgets, staff, and authority over efficiently delivering public services. Departments may resist cross-agency collaboration or innovation if it threatens their autonomy or exposes weaknesses. Metrics that emphasize compliance over outcomes encourage behavior that maintains the status quo rather than addressing societal needs. By realigning incentives to reward impact, accountability, and collaboration, governments can transform bureaucracies into service-oriented organizations. Predictable human behavior ensures that when incentives reward survival over service, bureaucracies will optimize for themselves. Effective policy implementation depends on reconfiguring these structural incentives.

Historical examples highlight the persistence of bureaucratic self-preservation. Large empires, early industrial administrations, and colonial governments often focused on maintaining authority, control, and resources rather than serving populations efficiently. Departments that expanded reporting requirements, internal audits, or administrative complexity protected themselves but created inefficiency and corruption. Modern bureaucracies display similar patterns if incentives favor internal security over mission fulfillment. Understanding this dynamic allows leaders to intervene and redesign systems that encourage service-oriented behavior. Incentive-aware leadership transforms institutions from self-preserving entities into effective problem-solving organizations.

Even personal and organizational processes mirror bureaucratic incentives. Teams, committees, or workgroups often optimize for visibility, approval, and resource acquisition rather than productive output. Individuals may spend more time protecting their roles than contributing meaningfully to outcomes. By aligning incentives with tangible results, recognition, and collaboration, leaders encourage behavior that prioritizes collective objectives over personal or departmental preservation. Predictable patterns emerge when humans respond to incentives: what is rewarded is what will be pursued. Designing incentive structures that emphasize service, value creation, and accountability transforms bureaucratic tendencies into productive, mission-focused outcomes.

Financial and corporate systems further illustrate the survival-over-service dynamic. Departments that protect revenue streams, budgets, or departmental status may resist efficiency improvements, cross-functional cooperation, or innovation. Risk-averse behavior is incentivized when stability and security are rewarded more than meaningful contribution or results. Redesigning incentives to prioritize outcomes, accountability, and value creation encourages teams to focus on effective performance rather than internal preservation. Employees and leaders respond predictably to what is rewarded and penalized within a system. Aligning bureaucratic incentives with purpose ensures that institutional behavior produces societal, organizational, and customer benefit rather than self-interest.

Public administration demonstrates similar challenges. Social service agencies, health departments, and regulatory bodies often prioritize visibility, compliance metrics, and procedural adherence over tangible outcomes for the public. Employees, managers, and executives rationally focus on the behaviors that maintain authority, budgets, and reputations. By structuring incentives to reward measurable improvements, citizen satisfaction, and effective problem-solving, governments can redirect bureaucratic behavior toward service. Systems function predictably when incentives are misaligned or aligned. Recognizing that bureaucracies optimize for survival allows policymakers to redesign structures for public benefit. Incentive-aware governance transforms self-preserving systems into results-driven organizations.

Innovation and reform within bureaucracies require a deliberate redesign of incentives. Agencies and organizations must balance risk management with outcomes, reward collaboration, and measure impact rather than mere activity. Leaders who understand how individuals respond to incentive structures can implement changes that shift focus from survival to mission fulfillment. Departments naturally gravitate toward the behaviors that are rewarded, making structural incentives critical for alignment. By creating reward systems for impact, efficiency, and collaboration, bureaucracies become capable of serving their intended purpose. Incentive design is therefore central to overcoming institutional inertia and fostering effective governance.

Finally, mastering bureaucratic incentive design requires both observation and intervention. Leaders, reformers, and policymakers must identify the behaviors that current incentives encourage and restructure systems to reward desired outcomes. Self-preservation will always be present, but when balanced with purpose-driven rewards, bureaucracies can optimize for service rather than mere survival. Predictable responses to incentives make systemic reform achievable when aligned with desired objectives. Aligning bureaucratic behavior with mission ensures that institutions fulfill their intended role efficiently, ethically, and sustainably. Redesigning incentives transforms bureaucracies from inward-focused entities into outward-serving engines of value.

Chapter .19

Corruption Is Predictable Under Certain Incentive Structures

Corruption flourishes when personal rewards exceed the cost of accountability.

Corruption is rarely a matter of individual moral failure alone; it is often a rational response to the incentives present within a system. When the rewards for unethical behavior—financial gain, power, or influence—outweigh the perceived risks or penalties, individuals act predictably in their self-interest. Organizations, governments, and institutions that fail to align incentives with ethical conduct inadvertently create fertile ground for corruption. Understanding this dynamic allows policymakers, corporate leaders, and reformers to anticipate and prevent corrupt behavior. Systems, not only morality, determine the prevalence of corruption. Redesigning incentives to balance reward and accountability is essential to reducing systemic corruption.

Corporate environments provide clear examples of incentive-driven corruption. Executives and managers may manipulate financial statements, exploit loopholes, or engage in bribery when personal gain is substantial and oversight is weak. Sales teams may prioritize bonuses over ethical considerations, cutting corners to achieve targets. Employees respond predictably to the incentives they face, acting in ways that maximize personal or departmental advantage. Organizations that redesign incentives to reward ethical behavior, transparency, and long-term value creation reduce opportunities for corruption. Predictable human behavior ensures that incentives drive actions more reliably than moral exhortation alone. Ethical culture emerges when the system rewards integrity over exploitation.

Government institutions and public policy are similarly shaped by incentive structures. Officials may embezzle funds, award contracts unfairly, or abuse authority when enforcement is weak and personal gain is high. Bureaucrats respond to the incentives embedded in their roles, prioritizing behaviors that increase wealth, influence, or political advantage. Regulatory gaps, opaque processes, and weak accountability mechanisms magnify the problem. By designing systems that reward transparency, long-term performance, and public benefit while penalizing misconduct, corruption can be anticipated and mitigated. Predictable responses to incentives make structural reform the most effective tool against corrupt behavior. Aligning incentives with public service strengthens governance and societal trust.

Historical examples illustrate how incentive misalignment fosters corruption. Colonial administrations, monopolistic enterprises, and early financial institutions often experienced widespread corruption because personal enrichment opportunities exceeded the cost of exposure. In contrast, organizations and governments that implemented clear rules, independent oversight, and reward systems aligned with mission objectives experienced lower levels of unethical behavior. These cases highlight that corruption is systemic, not merely individual. When personal gain is unchecked and accountability is weak, rational actors exploit the system. Leaders who anticipate this dynamic can proactively design incentives to prevent corruption.

Even personal and local organizations are influenced by these dynamics. Small businesses, nonprofit boards, or community projects may face predictable misbehavior if individuals see personal gain exceeding the risk of scrutiny. Volunteers, employees, or managers respond to the incentives embedded in their environment, often prioritizing self-interest over collective outcomes. By designing systems that balance rewards, recognition, and accountability, leaders ensure that ethical behavior is the rational choice. Incentive-aware management prevents corruption from emerging at any scale. Recognizing predictable patterns of behavior allows leaders to structure systems that naturally discourage unethical actions.

Financial systems demonstrate the consequences of misaligned incentives vividly. Traders, investment managers, and executives may engage in risky or fraudulent practices when bonuses, stock options, or personal wealth accumulation exceed the perceived cost of legal or reputational risk. Misaligned reward structures can produce crises, scandals, and systemic instability. Redesigning incentive systems to align performance metrics with ethical standards, transparency, and long-term outcomes reduces corruption and promotes stability. Investors and employees act predictably in response to incentives, making structural reform essential. Ethical outcomes are achieved not solely through enforcement but by ensuring that integrity is rewarded more than opportunism.

Corporate and nonprofit boards illustrate the importance of incentive oversight. Without performance measures tied to ethical behavior, transparency, and stakeholder benefit, executives may pursue self-serving actions. Predictable responses to incentives make governance structures critical in shaping behavior. Boards that integrate accountability, audits, and clear reward systems ensure that integrity aligns with personal and organizational success. Incentives that reward ethical contributions and penalize misconduct shape behavior at every organizational level. Misalignment of incentives produces corruption, whereas thoughtful design promotes predictable ethical action.

Public sector reform highlights strategies to prevent corruption. Implementing transparency initiatives, independent oversight, and performance-based accountability changes the incentives for officials and agencies. When opportunities for personal enrichment are minimized and consequences for misconduct are visible and meaningful, corruption decreases. Citizens respond predictably to the systems in which they operate, as do leaders, administrators, and bureaucrats. Aligning incentives with public benefit ensures that ethical behavior is both rational and rewarding. Structural design, rather than moral exhortation, is the most reliable tool to combat systemic corruption.

Finally, mastering incentive design to prevent corruption requires understanding predictable human behavior. Individuals naturally pursue rewards and avoid penalties, meaning systems must align these forces with ethical objectives. Leaders, organizations, and governments that structure incentives to reward integrity, transparency, and long-term value reduce opportunities for corruption. Misaligned incentives, by contrast, encourage predictable unethical behavior even among otherwise moral actors. By anticipating how people respond to rewards and consequences, systems can be designed to minimize corruption and maximize societal benefit. Ethical behavior emerges as a rational choice when incentives are thoughtfully aligned with public and organizational interest.

Chapter .20

Democracy Works Best When Incentives Favor Long-Term Stewardship

Political systems improve when leaders are rewarded for lasting outcomes rather than short-term wins.

Democracy functions optimally when political incentives encourage leaders to focus on sustainable, long-term outcomes rather than immediate popularity or short-term gains. Politicians naturally respond to the structures that reward visibility, reelection, and approval ratings, often prioritizing superficial victories over substantive policy. Aligning incentives with stewardship encourages decision-making that benefits future generations, strengthens institutions, and addresses systemic challenges. Understanding how incentive structures shape political behavior is essential for creating resilient democratic systems. When long-term outcomes are valued, leaders act predictably in ways that advance societal stability. Redesigning democratic incentives ensures that governance prioritizes enduring progress rather than transient popularity.

Electoral structures strongly influence whether leaders prioritize stewardship or short-term wins. Systems emphasizing frequent elections, popularity contests, or media visibility cncourage politicians to focus on immediate appeal, often at the expense of sustainable policies. Conversely, electoral frameworks that reward consistent, evidence-based progress and long-term performance encourage leaders to plan beyond the next cycle. Citizens, parties, and policymakers respond predictably to these incentives, shaping the behavior of elected officials. Institutional design that aligns rewards with lasting outcomes promotes predictable, responsible governance. Democracy thrives when incentives reward careful planning and enduring societal benefit.

Government bureaucracies and civil institutions also reflect these dynamics. Agencies, departments, and officials optimize for the behaviors that are rewarded within their systems, which may prioritize budget preservation, political alignment, or procedural compliance over long-term impact. Policies and programs that incentivize collaboration, innovation, and sustainability produce outcomes that align with democratic ideals. By designing performance metrics, recognition systems, and accountability mechanisms around long-term results, governments can ensure that bureaucratic behavior supports stewardship. Leaders and civil servants act predictably in response to incentives, making structural design a powerful lever for effective governance. Sustainable democracy depends on aligning institutional incentives with societal outcomes.

Historical examples reveal the consequences of misaligned incentives in democratic systems. Short-termism has contributed to fiscal crises, environmental degradation, and policy instability across nations, as leaders prioritized immediate approval over strategic planning. Conversely, nations and municipalities that embedded long-term planning and accountability in their democratic structures produced enduring institutions, stable economies, and social progress. Incentive structures shaped these outcomes more reliably than ideology, charisma, or moral persuasion. Leaders naturally optimize for the behaviors rewarded by the system, demonstrating the predictive power of incentives. Democracies succeed when the structures reward stewardship rather than superficial popularity.

Even at the local and personal level, democratic stewardship relies on incentive alignment. Community boards, councils, and local governments respond to metrics of recognition, funding, and influence, often optimizing for visibility rather than long-term impact. By designing incentives that reward measurable outcomes, collaboration, and sustainable solutions, local leaders produce benefits for their constituents. Citizens, volunteers, and administrators adjust behavior predictably based on the rewards and consequences they perceive. Democracy is strengthened when these incentives are structured to favor service, accountability, and impact over short-term approval. Incentive design at every level fosters a culture of responsible, long-term governance.

Financial, corporate, and nonprofit systems mirror the same principle. Boards, executives, and managers respond to incentives embedded in governance, prioritizing visible achievements or short-term metrics over sustainable growth. By aligning rewards with long-term impact, ethical behavior, and strategic planning, institutions can produce outcomes that mirror the benefits of stewardship in democratic systems. Leaders and employees act predictably according to the incentives they face, demonstrating the universality of this principle. Incentives that reward foresight, responsibility, and sustainable outcomes cultivate predictable, beneficial behavior across sectors. Democracy, like organizations, thrives when long-term stewardship is incentivized.

Media and public opinion also shape democratic incentives. Politicians respond to coverage, public sentiment, and polling, which often emphasize immediate, emotional, or controversial issues. When media and societal rewards prioritize short-term attention, leaders act predictably to capture visibility rather than deliver sustainable policy. By designing systems that reward thoughtful deliberation, evidence-based decisions, and accountability, media and public engagement can support long-term democratic stewardship. Incentives guide behavior in predictable ways, making alignment essential for positive outcomes. Democracy works best when all actors—leaders, citizens, and institutions—respond to incentives that favor lasting impact.

Innovation and reform in democratic systems require deliberate incentive design. Policymakers, voters, and civil servants must ensure that recognition, funding, and career advancement reward long-term outcomes rather than immediate wins. Systems that align incentives with stewardship foster predictable, positive behavior and strengthen institutional resilience. When leaders are rewarded for sustainable policies, risk-taking, and collaboration, democratic systems adapt effectively to evolving challenges. Incentives act as the behavioral guideposts for governance, ensuring that decisions prioritize enduring societal benefit. Structuring democratic incentives around stewardship transforms governance from reactive short-termism into proactive long-term progress.

Finally, mastering incentive design for democracy requires understanding predictable human behavior. Leaders, institutions, and citizens naturally optimize for what is rewarded, making systemic alignment critical. By embedding long-term stewardship into electoral systems, bureaucracies, public accountability mechanisms, and civic engagement structures, democracies can produce predictable, beneficial outcomes. Short-term popularity should be balanced with incentives that reward foresight, planning, and responsibility. Predictable political behavior emerges when incentives favor sustainable governance over immediate approval. Aligning democratic incentives with long-term stewardship ensures resilient, effective, and enduring systems for the benefit of all.

Part V — Incentives in Culture, Media, and Technology

CHAPTER .21

MEDIA INCENTIVES REWARD OUTRAGE OVER TRUTH

Attention-based business models prioritize emotional reactions over accuracy.

Modern media operates in a highly competitive environment where attention drives revenue, influence, and survival. Platforms, publishers, and journalists respond predictably to incentives that prioritize clicks, shares, and engagement over factual accuracy. Content that provokes strong emotional reactions—especially outrage—tends to spread faster, generating measurable rewards. As a result, sensationalized or misleading information often receives greater visibility than nuanced, accurate reporting. Understanding how incentive structures shape media behavior is essential for consumers, policymakers, and media leaders seeking reliable information. Redesigning incentives can encourage truth, accountability, and responsible journalism.

Corporate media organizations illustrate these dynamics clearly. News outlets often measure success in terms of page views, social engagement, and advertising revenue, leading to coverage that favors sensationalism over substance. Journalists and editors respond predictably to the rewards embedded in these systems, producing content that maximizes attention rather than insight. Social media algorithms amplify emotionally charged content because it generates engagement and ad revenue. Media companies that align incentives with accuracy, relevance, and quality reporting encourage responsible journalism while still maintaining profitability. Predictable responses to incentives explain why misinformation and clickbait dominate contemporary media landscapes. Properly aligned incentives reward rigorous, ethical reporting over sensationalism.

Government and public policy interact with media incentives in ways that shape society. Politicians and institutions often exploit media systems that reward outrage to influence public opinion, drive narratives, or gain visibility. Citizens respond to emotionally charged messaging, often forming beliefs or making decisions based on amplified content rather than verified facts. Media incentives create predictable behavioral patterns among audiences, leaders, and journalists alike. By structuring rewards for accuracy, transparency, and verification, societies can encourage more responsible information dissemination. Misaligned media incentives are not only a corporate issue—they influence governance, public perception, and civic behavior. Aligning media incentives with truth improves decision-making and societal outcomes.

Historical examples highlight the consequences of misaligned media incentives. Tabloid journalism, yellow press campaigns, and sensational reporting have historically shaped public opinion, policy, and even conflict by prioritizing attention over accuracy. The consequences include misinformation, polarization, and poor decision-making, illustrating how incentives drive predictable behavior. Societies that encouraged accountability, fact-checking, and responsible reporting achieved more stable and informed public discourse. Understanding that media behavior is largely incentive-driven allows reformers and leaders to predict and guide content quality. Aligning incentives with factual reporting fosters trust, stability, and informed decision-making. Incentive-aware media policy shapes both the production and consumption of news.

Even at a personal and community level, incentives influence information behavior. Individuals often share content that elicits strong emotional reactions to gain attention, approval, or social validation. Social recognition, likes, and comments act as rewards, reinforcing the sharing of sensational or misleading material.

Communities respond predictably to these incentives, amplifying content that maximizes engagement rather than accuracy. By consciously designing incentives—such as rewarding thoughtful discussion, verification, and critical thinking—social networks, workplaces, and educational systems can improve information quality. Predictable human behavior demonstrates that incentive structures shape both content creation and consumption. Aligning rewards with truth rather than outrage fosters more rational and responsible information ecosystems.

Technology companies and algorithms exemplify how incentives shape media behavior. Platforms that monetize attention have built-in rewards for content that provokes outrage, drives debate, or triggers strong reactions. Content creators respond predictably, producing material designed to maximize visibility and revenue. Algorithmic reinforcement of sensational content increases polarization, spreads misinformation, and diminishes public trust. Designing technological and financial incentives that prioritize accuracy, quality engagement, and responsible dissemination can guide creators toward productive outcomes. Predictable behavior emerges when systems reward what is measurable—attention, engagement, and impact. Properly aligned incentives in media transform information ecosystems from sensationalized and divisive to accurate and constructive.

Financial and business pressures further reinforce sensationalized media. Advertising revenue, subscription models, and investor expectations reward engagement metrics rather than journalistic rigor. Companies, editors, and content creators act predictably to optimize for these rewards, often at the expense of accuracy and depth. Conversely, media organizations that reward long-form reporting, verification, and informative storytelling cultivate credibility, trust, and sustained audience loyalty. Incentives shape behavior more powerfully than editorial directives or ethical exhortations alone. By aligning media rewards with truth, impact, and quality, organizations produce predictable improvements in content integrity. Incentive design transforms media ecosystems from reactive and sensational to informed and responsible.

Policy interventions can also reshape media incentives. Fact-checking initiatives, transparency requirements, and content moderation policies create structures where truth is rewarded and misinformation carries consequences. Citizens, platforms, and journalists respond predictably to these incentives, changing the information landscape over time. Misaligned incentives, by contrast, perpetuate sensationalism, polarization, and mistrust. Structural interventions that reward verification, accountability, and responsible reporting create sustainable improvement in media behavior. Understanding the predictive power of incentives allows policymakers and organizations to influence content quality effectively. Aligning media incentives with truth strengthens both information integrity and societal decision-making.

Finally, mastering media incentive design requires understanding human attention, motivation, and reward systems. Individuals, institutions, and organizations naturally optimize for what is rewarded, whether attention, revenue, or engagement. By structuring incentives that reward accuracy, verification, and responsible reporting, societies can predictably improve the quality of media. Misaligned incentives explain the proliferation of sensationalism, but deliberate alignment fosters trustworthy, informative, and constructive content. Proper incentive design transforms media from a source of division and distortion into a platform for truth, insight, and meaningful engagement. Predictable behavior emerges when rewards match desired outcomes, making incentive-aware design essential for media integrity.

Chapter .22

Social Media Trains Us to Perform, Not Reflect

Algorithmic incentives shape identity, behavior, and social norms.

Social media platforms operate on algorithms that reward engagement, visibility, and virality, creating a system where users are incentivized to perform for attention rather than reflect deeply on ideas or values. Likes, shares, and comments provide immediate feedback, encouraging behaviors that maximize public approval instead of thoughtful consideration. Users quickly learn to tailor their posts, opinions, and actions to the metrics that gain recognition, often sacrificing authenticity, nuance, or introspection. Understanding the incentive structures of social media is essential for individuals, organizations, and policymakers seeking to foster meaningful engagement. Systems reward performance, not reflection, producing predictable behavioral patterns. Redesigning these incentives can shift focus from superficial validation to constructive, thoughtful participation.

Corporate and platform examples illustrate this effect. Influencers, content creators, and brands optimize their posts for likes, shares, and algorithmic amplification rather than depth, learning, or ethical impact. Engagement-driven incentives encourage sensationalism, repetition, and emotional provocation, shaping both content and user behavior. Users respond predictably to these systems, performing in ways that maximize rewards rather than exploring ideas critically. Platforms that integrate incentives for constructive dialogue, long-form engagement, and fact-based content encourage reflection alongside performance. Incentive-aware design produces more meaningful interaction, mitigating the performative bias inherent in social media. Organizations and individuals must understand these dynamics to navigate digital environments effectively.

Government and policy actors are also influenced by social media performance incentives. Politicians, advocacy groups, and public institutions optimize messaging to gain immediate attention rather than encourage deliberation or long-term understanding. Citizens respond to visibility and emotional resonance, shaping public discourse in predictable ways. Misaligned incentives amplify polarization, misinformation, and performative behavior at the societal level. By creating policies and norms that reward verified information, thoughtful dialogue, and civic responsibility, societies can redirect predictable behaviors toward constructive outcomes. Understanding social media as an incentive system clarifies why performative engagement often dominates public discourse. Aligning incentives with reflection encourages deeper understanding and more informed participation.

Historical examples reveal the evolution of performative behavior in public communication. Public speaking, print media, and broadcast platforms also incentivized visibility, applause, and circulation, but social media accelerates and quantifies these rewards. Instant feedback loops and algorithmic reinforcement amplify attention-driven behaviors, making performative tendencies more predictable and pervasive. Users, organizations, and leaders adapt to these structures, often prioritizing visibility over substance. Recognizing this dynamic allows for interventions that encourage reflection, critical thinking, and responsible content creation. Incentive redesign is key to shifting the balance from performance-focused behavior to meaningful engagement.

Even personal and community behavior is shaped by these incentives. Individuals curate online personas to attract approval, often exaggerating achievements, opinions, or experiences. Peer feedback, social validation, and algorithmic rewards reinforce this performative behavior. Communities respond predictably, prioritizing visible engagement over thoughtful interaction or self-reflection. By consciously redesigning personal habits, social norms, and platform incentives, individuals can foster reflective behavior alongside visibility. Encouraging reflective practices—such as thoughtful posting, delayed engagement, and critical evaluation—aligns human behavior with deeper understanding rather than mere performance. Incentive-aware self-management produces more meaningful and balanced social media experiences.

Financial and business models reinforce performative behavior. Advertising, sponsorship, and content monetization reward virality, attention, and shareability, creating predictable pressures on content creators. Platforms, creators, and brands respond rationally, optimizing for engagement over authenticity or insight. By realigning financial incentives to reward educational, informative, or socially constructive content, systems can guide behavior toward reflective outcomes. Predictable behavioral responses make incentive redesign a powerful tool for shaping media quality and user engagement. When reflection is rewarded alongside visibility, social media can support both attention and depth. Aligning incentives transforms the digital landscape into a platform that values substance alongside performance.

Education and organizational environments reflect similar dynamics. Training programs, workplace communication tools, and collaborative platforms often reward visible participation over thoughtful contribution. Employees and students learn to perform, submitting the expected outputs rather than engaging in reflection or critical problem-solving. By adjusting incentives to reward insight, collaboration, and innovative thinking, leaders can counteract performative tendencies. Predictable behavior ensures that what is rewarded is what will be pursued, whether in classrooms, organizations, or social media. Incentive-aware design encourages reflection while maintaining engagement and productivity. Systems that balance performance and reflection produce more thoughtful, capable participants.

Technology platforms further shape societal norms through predictable incentive structures. Algorithms that reward sensationalism, repetition, or emotional impact reinforce behaviors that prioritize performance over reflection. Communities adapt to these incentives, internalizing behaviors that maximize visibility rather than thoughtful engagement. By redesigning algorithms, reward structures, and feedback loops, platforms can promote critical thinking, self-reflection, and informed dialogue. Predictable responses to incentives ensure that system design drives user behavior at scale. Incentive-aware technological design fosters constructive, reflective, and engaged digital communities.

Finally, mastering social media incentives requires understanding the human response to visibility, approval, and recognition. Users, organizations, and policymakers naturally optimize behavior based on rewards, making alignment crucial for meaningful outcomes. Incentive-aware design can balance performance and reflection, encouraging critical thinking, ethical engagement, and thoughtful participation. Misaligned incentives predictably produce performative, shallow behavior, while deliberate alignment fosters insight and depth. Social media systems, like all human systems, respond predictably to incentives, making thoughtful design essential. By aligning rewards with reflection and substance, digital platforms can cultivate meaningful engagement that benefits individuals, communities, and society.

Chapter .23

Technology Is Neutral Until Incentives Activate It

Tools become destructive or beneficial depending on the incentives guiding their use.

Technology itself is inherently neutral; it does not possess intent or morality. The outcomes it produces—whether positive or negative—depend entirely on the incentives surrounding its development, deployment, and use. Engineers, organizations, and governments respond predictably to rewards, penalties, and recognition, shaping how technology is applied in real-world contexts. Tools that are incentivized for efficiency, profit, or engagement may amplify harmful behavior, while those incentivized for social good, safety, or ethical impact promote beneficial outcomes. Understanding this dynamic is essential for business leaders, policymakers, and individuals navigating technological ecosystems. Incentives determine whether technology serves humanity or exacerbates problems.

Corporate technology examples illustrate this principle clearly. Social media platforms, AI-driven algorithms, and automation tools often prioritize engagement, clicks, and monetization over societal benefit. Employees, developers, and managers respond rationally to these reward structures, producing products that maximize attention or revenue rather than ethical or sustainable impact. Conversely, companies that align incentives with safety, transparency, and long-term value create technology that benefits society while remaining commercially viable. Predictable behavior ensures that incentives, not intentions, drive outcomes in technology. Thoughtful design of incentive structures transforms neutral tools into powerful instruments for positive change.

Government policy and regulation play a crucial role in activating technology's effects. Autonomous systems, surveillance tools, or biotech innovations respond to the rules, oversight, and incentives imposed by public institutions. When incentives prioritize safety, ethical standards, and public benefit, technology is deployed responsibly and equitably. Misaligned incentives, such as regulatory gaps or perverse subsidies, lead to misuse, exploitation, and societal harm. Policymakers and regulators can predictably influence behavior by structuring incentives that reward ethical, safe, and innovative application. Aligning incentives with long-term social goals ensures that technological development produces constructive outcomes rather than unintended consequences.

Historical examples demonstrate how neutral technologies take the direction of incentives. The printing press facilitated both education and propaganda; industrial machinery enabled both mass production and exploitative labor; the internet promotes knowledge while also spreading misinformation. These examples reveal that the potential of technology is realized or corrupted based on the surrounding incentive structure. Developers, users, and institutions adapt behavior to match the rewards they receive, illustrating the predictability of incentive-driven outcomes. Recognizing the centrality of incentives allows societies to guide technology toward positive impact. Neutral tools become either enablers of progress or instruments of harm depending on how they are incentivized.

Even personal and organizational adoption of technology is shaped by incentives. Employees using productivity software, students engaging with educational platforms, or individuals interacting with social media respond predictably to the incentives embedded in these systems. Features that reward speed, quantity, or visibility often produce shallow engagement or counterproductive habits. Conversely, incentives that reward quality, learning, collaboration, and ethical use encourage positive behavior and skill development. Predictable human responses to technology highlight the need for conscious incentive design at both micro and macro levels. Thoughtful alignment of incentives ensures that individuals and organizations extract maximum benefit from neutral tools.

Financial and market forces further determine how technology manifests in society. Investors, executives, and entrepreneurs pursue technologies that promise high returns, often creating pressure to prioritize speed, market dominance, or engagement over ethical considerations. Employees and developers respond predictably to these financial incentives, focusing on outcomes that maximize rewards. Conversely, funding structures, grants, or recognition that prioritize social impact, sustainability, or safety guide technological innovation toward beneficial outcomes. Incentive-aware investment and organizational design align behavior with the intended purpose of technology. Systems that consider incentives transform neutral tools into drivers of value rather than harm.

Organizational culture also shapes technology outcomes. Companies, nonprofits, and government institutions reward behaviors that optimize for specific metrics—efficiency, engagement, or compliance—shaping how technology is implemented and used. Employees respond rationally to these incentives, producing predictable patterns of adoption and application. Incentives that emphasize collaboration, ethical use, and long-term impact guide technology toward constructive ends. By consciously designing reward structures around desired outcomes, leaders can ensure that technology serves strategic objectives and societal good. Misaligned incentives, conversely, amplify misuse, exploitation, or harm. Understanding predictable responses to incentives is critical for effective technology management.

Education and skill development depend on incentivized technology use. Digital learning platforms, AI tutors, and simulation tools respond to the behaviors they are rewarded for encouraging. Students, instructors, and institutions respond predictably to these systems, focusing on outcomes that maximize engagement or measurable success rather than depth of learning or critical thinking. By designing incentives that reward mastery, creativity, and ethical problem-solving, technology becomes a tool for meaningful education. Predictable responses to incentive structures ensure that educational technology produces intended learning outcomes. Properly aligned incentives transform neutral tools into instruments that enhance knowledge, skill, and personal growth.

Finally, mastering incentive design around technology requires understanding human behavior, organizational dynamics, and systemic effects. Tools themselves are neutral, but predictable human responses to rewards and penalties determine whether outcomes are beneficial or harmful. Leaders, policymakers, and innovators must consciously align incentives with long-term, ethical, and sustainable goals. Misaligned incentives produce predictable misuse or harm, while thoughtful alignment guides behavior toward innovation, efficiency, and societal benefit. Neutral technologies only become powerful enablers when incentives activate them toward positive, purposeful outcomes. Predictable human behavior makes incentive-aware design the critical factor in leveraging technology effectively.

Chapter .24

Virality Is an Incentive That Distorts Reality

Content spreads fastest when incentives reward shock rather than substance.

Virality has become a dominant force in modern media, driven by platforms and algorithms that reward engagement above all else. Users, creators, and organizations respond predictably to incentives that maximize reach, attention, and shares, often prioritizing sensationalism over accuracy or depth. The pursuit of viral content encourages exaggeration, misrepresentation, and simplification, which can distort public perception and decision-making. Understanding the incentive dynamics behind virality is essential for consumers, businesses, and policymakers seeking to maintain truth and clarity in communication. Systems that reward shock, novelty, and emotional impact produce predictable behaviors that can amplify misinformation. Aligning incentives with substance over sensation reduces distortion and promotes more rational engagement.

Corporate examples demonstrate how virality drives content strategy. Social media teams, marketers, and brand managers optimize for shareable, emotionally charged content that attracts clicks, likes, and attention. Employees and content creators naturally adjust behavior to maximize engagement metrics, producing predictable patterns of exaggeration, sensationalism, and emotional manipulation. Platforms amplify content that aligns with these incentives, further distorting reality in the public eye. Companies that intentionally reward quality, verification, and meaningful storytelling foster predictable improvements in content integrity. Incentives shape behavior more reliably than moral exhortation or editorial directives alone. Designing reward structures for substance rather than virality produces measurable benefits for audiences and organizations alike.

Government and policy arenas are similarly affected by virality incentives. Politicians, public agencies, and advocacy groups respond to platforms that amplify emotionally charged or controversial content. Campaigns, policies, and messaging may be shaped to maximize visibility, even if accuracy, nuance, or long-term outcomes are compromised. Citizens respond predictably to viral narratives, forming opinions and making decisions based on distorted information rather than facts. Policymakers and institutions can counteract these effects by designing incentives that reward verified information, transparency, and long-term impact. Misaligned incentive structures amplify sensationalism, while proper alignment encourages responsible communication. Understanding virality as a predictable outcome of incentives helps leaders reduce distortion and improve public discourse.

Historical examples highlight the consequences of viral incentive structures. Rumors, pamphlets, and sensational journalism have long spread information that was exaggerated or misleading, shaping public perception, policy, and behavior. Modern virality accelerates these dynamics exponentially, as algorithms and global connectivity magnify the speed and reach of content. Predictable responses to attention-based rewards drive behavior at all levels—from individual users to large institutions. Recognizing that virality is a function of incentive design allows organizations and policymakers to intervene effectively. Aligning rewards with accuracy and substance mitigates predictable distortions caused by attention-driven behavior. Incentive-aware design in communication systems fosters clarity, trust, and informed decision-making.

Even personal and community behavior is shaped by viral incentives. Individuals often share content that provokes reactions, gains visibility, or signals alignment with social norms, rather than critically evaluating accuracy or relevance. Peer feedback, likes, and algorithmic amplification reinforce predictable patterns of sensationalized sharing. Communities respond to these incentives by amplifying content that maximizes attention, often misrepresenting reality. By creating incentives that reward verification, reflection, and meaningful engagement, individuals and groups can counteract the distortive effects of virality. Predictable responses to attention-based rewards demonstrate the need for conscious incentive design. Aligning social behavior with accuracy and substance improves information ecosystems at every scale.

Financial and business systems further reinforce virality-driven distortion. Advertising revenue, sponsorships, and platform monetization depend on attention, clicks, and shares, creating a predictable incentive to prioritize sensational content. Creators, marketers, and platforms naturally optimize for these rewards, often at the expense of truth or quality. By adjusting financial and recognition incentives to reward factual, meaningful, and constructive content, organizations can shift predictable behavior toward desirable outcomes. Incentive-aware systems guide creators and institutions to produce reliable, impactful content rather than simply chasing virality. Platforms and businesses that balance engagement with accuracy produce better outcomes for users, stakeholders, and society. Properly aligned incentives transform virality from a source of distortion into an opportunity for meaningful communication.

Organizational culture also shapes responses to virality incentives. Teams, institutions, and departments that reward attention over substance cultivate behaviors that exaggerate, sensationalize, or simplify messages. Employees respond predictably to the reward structures present, producing content that maximizes visibility while sacrificing depth. By designing internal incentives that prioritize insight, clarity, and factual communication, organizations guide behavior toward reliable outputs. Predictable human responses to incentive structures make organizational design a critical lever for reducing distortion. Rewarding substance over shock produces content and actions that align with mission, ethics, and long-term impact. Incentive-aware culture fosters both engagement and integrity across communication channels.

Education and professional development are influenced by virality-driven behavior as well. Students, trainees, and professionals often adapt to attention-based incentives, prioritizing recognition, shares, or popularity over learning, analysis, or reflection. Predictable behaviors emerge as participants optimize for visible rewards rather than substantive outcomes. Designing incentives that reward mastery, depth, collaboration, and critical thinking aligns behavior with long-term development. Platforms, institutions, and educators can counteract the distortive effects of viral incentives by structuring recognition and reward around quality, learning, and insight. Incentive-aware design in educational and professional settings cultivates reflective, capable, and responsible individuals. Aligning incentives ensures that performance and impact reinforce accuracy and understanding.

Finally, mastering virality as an incentive requires understanding human and systemic behavior. Content creators, users, and organizations respond predictably to rewards embedded in attention-based systems. Misaligned incentives produce distortion, sensationalism, and shallow engagement, while aligned incentives foster truth, clarity, and thoughtful communication. Structural interventions, financial incentives, and cultural norms can shift behavior toward meaningful outcomes. Recognizing that virality is driven by predictable responses to reward structures allows leaders to design systems that promote accuracy, integrity, and insight. Properly aligned incentives transform the viral potential of modern communication into a force for understanding, not distortion.

Chapter .25

Cultural Decline Follows Incentive Decay

Values erode when incentives reward appearances over integrity.

Culture is sustained not merely by ideals, traditions, or beliefs, but by the incentives embedded in social, organizational, and institutional systems. When behavior is rewarded based on appearance, conformity, or superficial success rather than genuine contribution and integrity, cultural decay follows predictably. Individuals and organizations respond rationally to the rewards they perceive, shaping behavior and social norms in ways that reinforce the incentive structure. Understanding this dynamic is critical for leaders, policymakers, and communities seeking to preserve meaningful cultural values. Incentives determine what is practiced, celebrated, and passed on, making them central to cultural health. Properly aligned rewards maintain the strength and vitality of societal norms and institutions.

Corporate culture provides a clear example of how incentive decay leads to decline. When promotions, recognition, or bonuses prioritize visibility, politicking, or short-term performance over collaboration, ethics, or innovation, organizational values erode. Employees respond predictably, optimizing for what is rewarded, which may conflict with long-term objectives or moral standards. Over time, these behaviors become normalized, reinforcing superficiality and undermining authenticity. Companies that design incentives around integrity, creativity, and meaningful contribution cultivate resilient, positive culture. Predictable human behavior ensures that cultural norms mirror the incentives embedded within organizational systems. Incentive alignment transforms corporate culture from performative to authentic and values-driven.

Governments and public institutions are also vulnerable to cultural decay when incentives misalign. Bureaucrats, policymakers, and officials often prioritize personal advancement, public image, or procedural compliance over societal benefit. Citizens and leaders respond predictably to these incentives, producing governance that emphasizes appearances rather than outcomes. Over time, institutions lose public trust and ethical grounding, as behavior reflects rewarded actions rather than shared values. Aligning incentives with accountability, transparency, and service reinforces cultural norms that support ethical governance. Predictable responses to systemic incentives make it possible to anticipate and prevent cultural erosion. Incentive-aware governance strengthens social cohesion and institutional legitimacy.

Historical examples illustrate how cultural decline follows incentive decay. Empires, corporations, and social movements that rewarded status, display, or symbolic achievements over substantive contribution often experienced moral and institutional erosion. Leaders and participants responded predictably, prioritizing behaviors that maximized reward rather than aligned with enduring values. Societies that designed incentive systems to reward meaningful achievement, ethical behavior, and societal contribution maintained cultural strength and cohesion. Misaligned incentives, by contrast, encourage superficiality, corruption, and decay over time. Recognizing the predictability of human response to incentives allows leaders to protect cultural values. Incentive design, not merely moral exhortation, determines whether cultural ideals endure or erode.

Even at the personal and community level, incentive structures shape behavior. Individuals naturally optimize for rewards embedded in social, professional, and familial systems, whether those rewards are recognition, status, or material gain. Communities respond predictably, elevating visible actions over genuine contribution when incentives favor appearances. By aligning incentives to reward integrity, learning, creativity, and meaningful engagement, leaders and families can preserve and strengthen cultural norms. Incentive-aware design ensures that values are practiced, reinforced, and transmitted across generations. Proper alignment creates a virtuous cycle where authentic behavior is rewarded and cultural decay is prevented. Predictable human behavior ensures that culture flourishes when incentives reflect the values we seek to uphold.

Financial and organizational pressures can accelerate cultural decay if incentives reward profit, visibility, or efficiency at the expense of ethics, sustainability, or collaboration. Employees and managers naturally adjust behavior to maximize what is rewarded, reinforcing short-term or performative norms. Companies that embed incentives for ethical decision-making, long-term impact, and collaborative success cultivate resilient culture and sustainable performance. Predictable responses to incentives make culture malleable and sensitive to reward structures. Designing systems that reinforce integrity and meaningful contribution ensures that cultural values are actively practiced. Incentive-aware leadership transforms cultural preservation from a theoretical ideal into a practical reality.

Education and professional development also reflect incentive-driven cultural outcomes. Students, teachers, and professionals adapt to reward systems, shaping norms, behaviors, and values within classrooms and organizations. Incentives that prioritize grades, certifications, or external validation over mastery, curiosity, and ethical engagement erode cultural commitment to learning and growth. By designing reward structures that recognize skill, creativity, and contribution, educators cultivate a culture of intellectual integrity and curiosity. Predictable behavior ensures that what is rewarded will shape the broader cultural landscape of learning institutions. Incentive alignment in education preserves the values of diligence, reflection, and knowledge transmission. Cultural decay can be mitigated when learning systems reward meaningful, not superficial, achievement.

Media and social systems magnify cultural decline when incentives favor spectacle over substance. Outrage, visibility, and performative acts are often rewarded more than reflection, accuracy, or contribution. Individuals and communities respond predictably to these incentive structures, adopting behaviors and norms that prioritize attention and image. Aligning incentives in social media, entertainment, and community recognition with authenticity, learning, and constructive engagement fosters cultural resilience. Predictable human behavior ensures that societal values reflect the incentives present in prominent platforms and institutions. Incentive-aware design guides cultural evolution toward integrity, substance, and long-term sustainability. When incentives reward authentic contribution, culture strengthens rather than erodes.

Finally, mastering cultural preservation requires understanding the predictive power of incentives. Individuals, organizations, and societies act according to the rewards and penalties embedded in their systems. Misaligned incentives predictably produce superficial, performative, or unethical behavior, leading to cultural decline. Properly aligned incentives encourage integrity, creativity, learning, and collaboration, reinforcing values across personal, organizational, and societal levels. Leaders, educators, policymakers, and influencers must consciously structure systems that reward substance over appearance. Predictable human responses make incentive-aware cultural design not only possible but necessary. When incentives reflect authentic values, culture flourishes, and societal norms strengthen rather than erode.

Part VI — Designing Better Incentive Systems

Chapter .26

Start With Behavior, Not Ideals

Effective systems are built by rewarding desired actions rather than declaring intentions.

Creating meaningful change requires focusing on observable behavior rather than abstract ideals or lofty intentions. Systems that reward intentions alone often fail because people act based on tangible incentives rather than moral exhortation. Organizations, governments, and individuals respond predictably to what is rewarded, making behavior the most reliable lever for producing desired outcomes. By designing incentives that reinforce specific actions aligned with goals, leaders can create predictable, positive change. Ideals provide direction, but behavior produces results, and incentives shape which behaviors dominate. Prioritizing actionable reinforcement over abstract values ensures that systems achieve their stated objectives.

Corporate environments illustrate the importance of starting with behavior. Employee performance, culture, and productivity improve when reward structures target specific, observable actions such as collaboration, innovation, or customer satisfaction. Recognizing effort or good intentions without linking them to measurable outcomes often leads to misaligned behaviors or gaming of the system. Employees respond predictably to the incentives provided, adjusting actions to maximize reward rather than uphold abstract ideals. Organizations that design incentive systems around clear behaviors foster sustainable performance, ethical conduct, and long-term success. Prioritizing behavior over ideals ensures that cultural and operational goals are realized. Rewarding action, not rhetoric, produces measurable and lasting results.

Governments and policy-making benefit from a similar approach. Regulations, programs, and initiatives often fail because they emphasize intended outcomes or broad ideals without designing incentives that guide concrete behavior. Citizens, bureaucrats, and officials respond predictably to what is rewarded, and systems that fail to align incentives with desired actions produce unintended consequences. Policies that specify and reward actionable behaviors—such as compliance, reporting, or collaboration—achieve more consistent results. Incentive-aware governance focuses on behavior as the practical expression of policy goals. Aligning rewards with action rather than abstract ideals creates more effective and accountable systems. Observable behavior provides a reliable metric for evaluating the success of policy interventions.

Historical examples demonstrate that societies and organizations that reward behavior rather than intentions produce predictable success. Military campaigns, public health initiatives, and economic reforms often succeeded when actions were clearly incentivized, not merely when leaders or citizens were motivated by ideals. Misaligned incentives that rewarded appearances or intentions over behavior often led to failure or stagnation. Leaders who understood the predictive power of behavior and designed systems accordingly achieved lasting impact. Predictable human responses to incentives demonstrate why focusing on actionable outcomes is more effective than emphasizing abstract goals. Incentive-aligned systems transform aspirational ideals into tangible results.

Personal development and community leadership also benefit from behavior-focused incentives. Individuals striving to improve skills, relationships, or habits often make progress when specific actions are rewarded rather than mere commitment or intent. Communities that reward contribution, consistency, and collaboration foster stronger engagement and shared norms. Predictable human behavior ensures that incentives targeting action produce the outcomes people desire. Leaders, mentors, and educators can guide personal and social growth by prioritizing observable behavior over abstract ideals. Aligning rewards with action strengthens systems at every scale, producing consistent, measurable improvement. Behavior-focused design ensures that good intentions translate into meaningful results.

Financial and business metrics further highlight the importance of behavior-focused incentives. Bonus structures, promotions, and recognition systems that reward specific performance behaviors, such as meeting customer needs or innovating processes, drive predictable improvement. Systems that reward intentions, promises, or visibility without tying them to concrete action often fail. Employees respond rationally to reward structures, emphasizing behaviors that maximize benefit. By designing incentives around observable actions rather than ideals, leaders can ensure alignment between goals, behavior, and outcomes. Predictable behavioral responses make action-focused incentives a cornerstone of effective organizational strategy. Behavior becomes the bridge between ambition and achievement when rewards are thoughtfully aligned.

Education and professional development follow the same principle. Students, trainees, and employees progress most effectively when reward structures focus on demonstrated behavior, such as mastery, collaboration, or problem-solving, rather than abstract effort or stated intentions. Individuals respond predictably to incentives, making measurable actions the most reliable guide for system design. Aligning feedback, recognition, and reward with specific behaviors ensures that learning, growth, and development are tangible and sustainable. Incentive-aware structures convert aspiration into achievement, transforming ideals into measurable progress. Systems that emphasize action over rhetoric produce better educational and professional outcomes. Observable behavior is the foundation on which meaningful development is built.

Technology adoption and innovation also demonstrate the power of behavior-focused incentives. Platforms, tools, and workflows are only effective when usage and engagement are aligned with desired outcomes. Rewarding intentions, enthusiasm, or adoption without linking incentives to effective behavior often leads to wasted resources or counterproductive outcomes. Users, developers, and organizations respond predictably to what is reinforced, highlighting the necessity of behavior-focused design. Aligning technological incentives with actionable behaviors produces reliable, scalable results. Predictable responses to structured incentives ensure that technology serves strategic objectives rather than superficial appearances. Focusing on behavior transforms tools into instruments of measurable impact.

Finally, mastering incentive design requires a consistent focus on behavior rather than ideals. People, organizations, and systems act predictably in response to rewards and penalties, making behavior the most reliable lever for change. Abstract ideals guide vision, but only actionable behavior produces measurable outcomes. By designing incentives around specific, observable actions, leaders create predictable, positive results across corporate, governmental, educational, and personal contexts. Incentive-aware systems convert intention into action, aspiration into achievement, and vision into measurable progress. Focusing on behavior ensures that ideals are realized in the real world, producing consistent, lasting impact.

CHAPTER .27

ALIGN INDIVIDUAL GAIN WITH COLLECTIVE GOOD

The strongest systems make doing the right thing the most rewarding option.

Sustainable success depends on designing systems where personal gain naturally aligns with collective benefit. When individuals see that their self-interest coincides with the group's success, behavior becomes predictable and constructive. Misaligned incentives, in contrast, create conflict, inefficiency, and unethical actions, as individuals pursue rewards at the expense of others. Leaders, organizations, and policymakers must structure incentives so that doing the right thing also maximizes personal advantage. Understanding this principle allows for the creation of predictable, high-functioning systems in business, government, and society. Aligning self-interest with shared goals transforms competition into cooperation and ensures enduring progress.

Corporate examples illustrate the power of aligned incentives. Profit-sharing programs, team-based bonuses, and performance rewards tied to company-wide success encourage employees to work collaboratively rather than competitively. When individuals see personal gain linked to organizational performance, they invest in behaviors that support colleagues, clients, and long-term business outcomes. Conversely, systems that reward individual achievement in isolation often produce cutthroat, short-termist behavior that undermines the collective mission. Employees respond predictably to the incentives embedded in their environment, demonstrating the critical role of alignment. Aligning individual gain with collective success fosters loyalty, innovation, and sustained organizational performance. Incentive-aware design ensures that doing the right thing benefits both the individual and the organization.

Government and policy-making provide parallel examples. Citizens, bureaucrats, and elected officials respond to incentive structures that balance personal benefit with societal good. Programs that reward civic participation, public service, or compliance with policies tied to measurable social outcomes create predictable, positive behaviors. Misaligned incentives, such as personal enrichment opportunities that conflict with public service, produce corruption, inefficiency, and distrust. By aligning personal benefit with societal improvement—through recognition, career advancement, or financial reward—governments can cultivate predictable, ethical, and effective action. Incentive design ensures that individuals maximize their gain by contributing to the public good. Predictable behavior emerges when self-interest and collective benefit converge.

Historical examples reinforce the importance of this principle. Cooperative societies, successful guilds, and thriving early organizations achieved stability when members recognized that personal success depended on collective contribution. Systems that misaligned personal and group rewards often experienced conflict, decline, or collapse. Leaders who understood the predictability of human response to incentives designed structures that aligned individual goals with collective outcomes. This principle applies across business, governance, and community settings, demonstrating universal relevance. Aligning incentives ensures that personal ambition becomes a force for shared prosperity rather than division. Incentive-aware design transforms self-interest into a catalyst for collective success.

Personal and community behavior also responds predictably to aligned incentives. Individuals are more likely to contribute time, effort, and resources to shared projects when they perceive that their actions benefit both themselves and the group. Families, neighborhoods, and volunteer organizations thrive when personal gain—recognition, fulfillment, or opportunity—is linked to the collective good. Misaligned incentives, by contrast, produce free-riding, selfish behavior, and disengagement. By consciously designing social systems and personal reward structures to balance self-interest with communal benefit, leaders and individuals foster predictable, cooperative behavior. Incentive-aware design ensures that individual ambition supports broader goals. Alignment transforms communities into collaborative, resilient networks.

Financial and organizational systems further highlight the value of aligned incentives. Shareholder profit, team-based compensation, and collaborative innovation programs all succeed when individual rewards reinforce collective goals. Employees, managers, and executives respond predictably to incentives, optimizing for behaviors that maximize both personal and organizational benefit. Misaligned systems—such as short-term bonuses disconnected from long-term value—produce predictable misbehavior, including risk-taking, exploitation, or ethical lapses. Structuring incentives to reward collective success alongside personal gain fosters loyalty, efficiency, and sustained growth. Incentive-aware design ensures that individual effort advances shared objectives, producing predictable, positive outcomes. Alignment converts potential conflicts into mutually reinforcing behaviors.

Education and professional development reflect the same principle. Students, teachers, and employees act predictably when their personal growth or recognition coincides with the success of peers, teams, or institutions. Collaborative projects, peer mentoring, and performance metrics tied to group achievement reinforce constructive behavior. Systems that reward individual achievement without regard for collective outcomes often foster unhealthy competition, disengagement, or knowledge hoarding. By aligning personal incentives with shared goals, leaders cultivate cooperative, high-performing learning and work environments. Predictable behavior emerges when self-interest and collective good converge. Incentive-aware design ensures that personal ambition enhances the group's success rather than undermining it.

Technology platforms and tools amplify the importance of alignment. Users, developers, and companies respond predictably to incentives embedded in systems, whether social, financial, or operational. Platforms that reward behaviors benefiting both the individual and the network—such as collaborative knowledge sharing, verified contributions, or ethical conduct—produce positive, predictable outcomes. Misaligned incentives, such as systems that reward attention at the expense of substance, create conflict, distortion, and harm. By designing technological incentives to align personal gain with collective success, systems can maximize both impact and engagement. Incentive-aware design ensures that neutral tools become instruments for cooperation and shared achievement. Alignment transforms technology into a vehicle for predictable, positive outcomes.

Finally, mastering the principle of aligning individual gain with collective good requires understanding predictable human behavior. Individuals, organizations, and institutions naturally optimize for what is rewarded, making system design a powerful lever. Misaligned incentives predictably produce conflict, short-termism, and unethical behavior, while aligned incentives produce cooperation, innovation, and enduring success. Leaders, policymakers, and educators can structure incentives so that doing the right thing becomes the most personally rewarding choice. Predictable human behavior ensures that alignment produces measurable, positive outcomes across all domains. Incentive-aware systems transform self-interest into a driving force for collective prosperity and societal progress.

Chapter .28

Make Long-Term Consequences Visible and Immediate

Delayed feedback weakens accountability and encourages harmful shortcuts.

People and organizations naturally prioritize immediate rewards over distant outcomes, often ignoring the long-term consequences of their actions. When consequences are delayed or abstract, predictable behaviors favor short-term gain, even at the expense of sustainability, ethics, or long-term success. Leaders, policymakers, and system designers must create structures that make future outcomes tangible and immediate. By linking visible, timely feedback to behavior, individuals and organizations respond predictably and make choices aligned with long-term objectives. Understanding this principle is crucial for driving sustainable success across business, governance, and personal development. Incentive-aware systems bridge the gap between present action and future impact, ensuring responsible behavior.

Corporate and organizational examples illustrate this concept clearly. Short-term performance metrics often encourage employees and managers to prioritize immediate results, ignoring long-term growth, innovation, or ethical considerations. Bonus structures tied solely to quarterly profits, for instance, can lead to risk-taking, cost-cutting, or corner-cutting that undermines long-term value. By contrast, organizations that design incentives with long-term feedback loops—such as deferred bonuses, equity rewards, or multi-year project evaluations—encourage behavior that benefits both the company and its stakeholders. Employees respond predictably to what is measured and rewarded, making long-term feedback essential. Aligning incentives with enduring outcomes strengthens culture, strategy, and resilience. Immediate visibility of long-term consequences ensures that choices consider both present and future impact.

Government and public policy also demonstrate the importance of visible consequences. Policies, regulations, and programs often fail because the long-term effects are abstract, delayed, or diffused across society. Bureaucrats, officials, and citizens respond predictably to the incentives presented by immediate feedback and recognition rather than distant outcomes. Structuring policy around tangible, timely measures—such as environmental impact reports, early-warning indicators, or phased accountability milestones—aligns behavior with long-term goals. Predictable responses to immediate feedback improve compliance, effectiveness, and sustainability. Incentive-aware policy design transforms abstract ideals into actionable, measurable results. Making consequences visible ensures responsible governance that anticipates future challenges rather than reacts belatedly.

Historical examples reveal the costs of ignoring long-term consequences. Financial collapses, environmental degradation, and social crises often emerged from systems that rewarded short-term gain while obscuring future costs. Leaders and institutions acted predictably, optimizing for immediate rewards without accounting for delayed effects. Conversely, civilizations, businesses, and communities that designed mechanisms to visualize and internalize long-term consequences produced more sustainable, resilient outcomes. Predictable human behavior demonstrates that delayed feedback undermines responsible action. Incentive-aware design ensures that long-term impacts are incorporated into present decision-making, producing stable and ethical systems. Making future consequences immediate prevents predictable shortsightedness and fosters foresight.

Personal and community behavior also responds to delayed or visible consequences. Individuals often prioritize immediate gratification over long-term goals, whether in health, finances, or relationships. Communities respond predictably to incentive structures, reinforcing behaviors that are rewarded immediately rather than sustainably. By designing systems that provide tangible, timely feedback—such as progress tracking, peer accountability, or visible rewards—leaders and individuals encourage choices aligned with long-term objectives. Predictable responses to visible consequences ensure that action considers both present and future implications. Incentive-aware design at personal and communal levels fosters habits, behaviors, and decisions that maximize enduring benefits. Making long-term consequences immediate bridges the gap between short-term behavior and sustainable outcomes.

Financial and market systems highlight this principle as well. Investors, executives, and employees often optimize for short-term metrics, producing predictable volatility, risk, or misalignment with long-term strategy. Deferred compensation, long-term performance evaluations, and visible outcome tracking align behavior with sustainable growth. Individuals respond predictably when the consequences of actions—positive or negative—are immediate and tangible. Misaligned incentives that obscure long-term effects foster predictable harmful behavior. By making consequences visible and actionable, leaders create systems where present actions naturally support future success. Incentive-aware design ensures that business decisions balance immediate rewards with enduring outcomes, producing stability and resilience.

Education and professional development reflect the same need for visible consequences. Students, trainees, and employees often prioritize immediate recognition, grades, or praise over mastery, skill acquisition, or ethical behavior. Predictable responses emerge when incentives favor short-term validation rather than sustained effort. By providing timely feedback, measurable milestones, and recognition linked to long-term achievement, educators and leaders align behavior with enduring goals. Individuals respond rationally to what is rewarded and visible, making immediate consequences a critical driver of success. Incentive-aware systems convert delayed outcomes into actionable feedback, fostering responsibility and growth. Making long-term impact tangible ensures predictable behavior that supports learning, mastery, and development.

Technology adoption and systems management demonstrate this principle at scale. Users, developers, and organizations respond predictably to incentives shaped by feedback loops. Features, dashboards, and analytics that visualize long-term effects—financial, environmental, or operational—encourage responsible use and alignment with strategic objectives. Misaligned incentives that hide or defer consequences foster misuse, inefficiency, or risk-taking. By making long-term impacts immediate and observable, leaders guide behavior toward constructive outcomes. Predictable human responses to incentives underscore the importance of visible feedback in complex systems. Incentive-aware design ensures that technology not only functions but drives behavior aligned with sustainable, long-term objectives.

Finally, mastering long-term consequence visibility requires a clear understanding of predictable human behavior. Individuals, organizations, and institutions naturally optimize for what is rewarded and visible. Delayed or abstract consequences produce predictable shortsightedness, while immediate, tangible feedback guides responsible action. Leaders, educators, and policymakers can design systems that link present behavior to future impact, ensuring accountability, foresight, and sustainability. Predictable responses to incentives allow alignment of short-term actions with long-term objectives across all domains. Making long-term consequences visible and immediate transforms abstract risks and benefits into actionable, reward-driven behavior. Incentive-aware design ensures that responsible, sustainable choices are both natural and predictable.

Chapter .29

Incentives Must Evolve as Systems Scale

What works in small systems often fails without adjustment at larger scales.

Incentives that succeed in small teams, organizations, or communities often fail when applied to larger systems. Human behavior remains predictable, but the complexity of interactions, feedback loops, and resource distribution changes as scale increases. Leaders, policymakers, and system designers must adjust incentives to reflect the dynamics of larger populations and more intricate networks. Misalignment at scale produces inefficiency, unintended consequences, and ethical lapses, even when the underlying principles are sound. Understanding how incentives interact with scale ensures that behavior continues to align with intended outcomes. Incentive-aware design requires constant adaptation to maintain effectiveness as systems grow.

Corporate examples illustrate the importance of scaling incentives. A startup may reward individual initiative and rapid iteration effectively, but as the company grows, these same rewards can encourage siloed behavior, miscommunication, or risk-taking that harms the organization. Larger organizations require structures that balance individual recognition with team performance, cross-functional collaboration, and strategic alignment. Employees respond predictably to incentives, so reward systems must evolve to guide behavior across more complex hierarchies and broader stakeholder networks. Failing to adjust incentives produces predictable dysfunction as systems expand. Thoughtful evolution of incentives ensures continued alignment of personal, team, and organizational goals. Scaling incentive design maintains performance, morale, and ethical behavior in growing organizations.

Government and policy systems face similar challenges. Policies that incentivize behavior effectively in local or regional contexts may fail when applied nationally or internationally. Citizens, bureaucrats, and institutions respond predictably to reward structures, so scaling requires adjustments to account for diverse populations, varying resources, and systemic interactions. Misaligned incentives at scale produce corruption, inefficiency, and unintended consequences, even when intentions are good. Designing multi-tiered incentives that account for local conditions, long-term outcomes, and interdependent systems maintains alignment and effectiveness. Predictable human behavior ensures that scalable incentives drive desired results across all levels. Incentive-aware governance adapts structures to preserve effectiveness and fairness as scale increases.

Historical examples reveal the consequences of failing to adapt incentives at scale. Empires, corporations, and social movements that expanded without adjusting reward structures often experienced dysfunction, misaligned behavior, and eventual collapse. Systems that worked well with a few participants failed to guide behavior predictably when thousands or millions were involved. Leaders who understood the need for adaptive incentives implemented governance, reporting, and accountability mechanisms that maintained alignment across growth. Predictable responses to rewards and penalties demonstrate that scaling requires intentional design. Incentive-aware systems ensure that expansion does not undermine effectiveness, ethics, or stability. Scaling without adaptation converts success into predictable failure.

Personal and community contexts also demonstrate the need for evolving incentives. A small team or neighborhood may thrive under informal recognition and peer accountability, but as groups grow, these incentives often lose effectiveness. Individuals respond predictably to what is rewarded, so larger communities require structured feedback, formal recognition, and systems that maintain alignment with collective goals. Failure to adapt leads to disengagement, conflict, and inefficiency. By designing incentives that evolve alongside system size, leaders and communities sustain cooperation, commitment, and ethical behavior. Predictable human behavior ensures that scalable incentive structures maintain desired outcomes. Incentive-aware adaptation prevents predictable decay as systems expand.

Financial and market systems illustrate the complexity of incentives at scale. Small-scale profit-sharing or project-based rewards function effectively within limited groups but can produce unintended consequences in large corporations, global supply chains, or financial markets. Employees, managers, and executives respond predictably to what is rewarded, making system-wide adaptation essential. Misaligned incentives in large systems can encourage short-termism, fraud, or resource misallocation. By scaling incentives thoughtfully—such as implementing multi-level rewards, long-term performance metrics, and accountability structures—organizations maintain alignment between individual action and collective goals. Predictable behavior ensures that well-designed incentives continue to produce desired outcomes regardless of system size. Incentive-aware design supports sustainable growth and ethical decision-making at scale.

Education and professional development also highlight the need for scalable incentives. Mentorship, recognition, and performance metrics effective in small classrooms or teams may fail in large universities or multinational organizations. Students, trainees, and employees respond predictably to what is rewarded, making adaptive systems necessary to maintain engagement and alignment. Incentives must account for diverse learners, distributed teams, and varying levels of expertise to sustain positive behavior. Systems that evolve with scale preserve motivation, collaboration, and ethical standards. Predictable human behavior allows leaders to design adaptive incentive frameworks that maintain performance and integrity as size increases. Incentive-aware scaling transforms small successes into large-scale, sustainable achievements.

Technology adoption and platform design further illustrate this principle. Features, algorithms, and reward systems that function effectively for a limited user base may produce unintended or harmful behaviors at scale. Users respond predictably to incentives, so design must evolve to address broader patterns, diverse populations, and complex interactions. Misaligned incentives at scale can create dysfunction, exploitation, or social harm. By continuously adapting feedback loops, rewards, and system parameters, technology can guide behavior predictably even in vast networks. Incentive-aware scaling ensures that platforms remain constructive, ethical, and effective regardless of growth. Aligning individual behavior with system goals across scale preserves both functionality and integrity.

Finally, mastering incentive evolution as systems scale requires understanding predictable human behavior and systemic complexity. Individuals, organizations, and communities act consistently in response to rewards and penalties, but interactions multiply and feedback loops change as systems grow. Misalignment at scale predictably produces dysfunction, inefficiency, and ethical lapses. By anticipating these dynamics and adjusting incentives, leaders, policymakers, and organizations maintain alignment, cooperation, and performance. Predictable behavior allows system designers to create adaptable, resilient frameworks that function effectively at any size. Incentive-aware scaling transforms small successes into sustainable, large-scale achievement and ensures long-term stability across complex systems.

CHAPTER .30

SIMPLICITY STRENGTHENS INCENTIVE CLARITY

Clear, understandable incentives outperform complex and opaque ones.

Simplicity in incentive design is essential for predictable, effective behavior. Complex, opaque, or overly nuanced rewards create confusion, loopholes, and unintended consequences, causing individuals and organizations to act in ways that undermine intended outcomes. People respond predictably to what they understand and can measure, making clarity a critical component of any incentive system. When incentives are simple, transparent, and easy to interpret, individuals align behavior naturally with desired goals. Overly complicated structures reduce comprehension, engagement, and trust. Incentive-aware design prioritizes clarity to ensure consistent, predictable results across personal, organizational, and societal contexts.

Corporate environments illustrate the power of simplicity. Employees respond more predictably to straightforward bonus structures, clear performance metrics, and transparent recognition programs. Complex systems with multiple overlapping rewards, convoluted rules, or unclear criteria produce gaming, confusion, and demotivation. Simple incentives align effort with outcomes, reinforcing behaviors that drive organizational success. Predictable human behavior ensures that what is rewarded will be pursued, and clarity maximizes the effectiveness of reward structures. Incentive clarity fosters trust, engagement, and sustainable performance. By prioritizing simplicity, leaders ensure that behavior is both directed and consistent.

Government and policy systems also benefit from clear incentives. Regulations, tax codes, and public programs often fail when they are overly complex, opaque, or difficult to interpret. Citizens, officials, and institutions respond predictably to incentives, but complexity reduces understanding and compliance. Simple, transparent policies encourage predictable behavior that aligns with public objectives. For example, straightforward tax incentives, clear penalties, or easy-to-understand social programs produce greater compliance and effectiveness. Incentive-aware design ensures that public behavior supports policy goals. Clarity reduces confusion, manipulation, and inefficiency, making systems more robust and fair.

Historical examples demonstrate the consequences of incentive complexity. Organizations, governments, and financial institutions that relied on opaque or convoluted reward structures often experienced misaligned behavior, corruption, and inefficiency. Complex rules and hidden rewards create predictable misinterpretation or exploitation. Societies and institutions that simplified incentives saw more consistent alignment between action and outcome. Predictable human behavior underscores the importance of designing rewards that are transparent and easily understood. Incentive clarity ensures that systems function as intended, reducing unintended consequences and promoting ethical behavior. Simple, comprehensible incentives strengthen both performance and accountability.

Personal and community behavior also responds to clarity in incentives. Individuals are more likely to pursue desired behaviors when the rewards are explicit, understandable, and directly linked to action. Ambiguous or hidden incentives produce confusion, inaction, or manipulation. Communities respond predictably to transparent structures, fostering cooperation, trust, and shared norms. By designing simple, clear incentive systems in families, neighborhoods, and social networks, leaders reinforce predictable, positive behavior. Incentive clarity transforms aspirations into action and ensures alignment between personal goals and community well-being. Simple rewards create predictable, consistent patterns of ethical, constructive behavior.

Financial and organizational systems further illustrate this principle. Investors, managers, and employees respond predictably to clear metrics, bonuses, and reward criteria. Complex compensation schemes, opaque performance reviews, or overlapping incentives reduce alignment and encourage gaming or short-termism. By designing simple, comprehensible incentive structures, organizations ensure that behavior aligns with strategic objectives. Predictable human behavior maximizes the value of transparent rewards, producing measurable outcomes. Incentive clarity also enhances trust and engagement, reinforcing organizational culture. Simplicity strengthens both efficiency and ethical alignment, ensuring that systems function as intended at scale.

Education and professional development benefit from simple, transparent incentives as well. Students, trainees, and employees respond predictably to clear grading systems, recognition programs, and performance metrics. Complex, opaque, or ambiguous reward structures reduce motivation, engagement, and learning outcomes. By emphasizing simplicity, educators and leaders create predictable pathways for growth and achievement. Clear incentives reinforce desired behaviors, ensuring that effort aligns with learning objectives and professional development goals. Predictable human behavior makes clarity a critical factor for educational success. Incentive-aware design transforms complexity into actionable, measurable, and sustainable progress.

Technology platforms and tools also demonstrate the importance of simplicity. Users, developers, and administrators respond predictably to rewards and feedback they can understand and measure. Complex, opaque algorithms or unclear reward structures lead to gaming, misuse, or disengagement. By simplifying feedback, performance metrics, and recognition systems, technology can guide behavior predictably and ethically. Incentive-aware design ensures that users act in ways aligned with system objectives and societal norms. Predictable behavior under simple structures fosters adoption, compliance, and positive impact. Simplicity strengthens system functionality while promoting responsible, goal-aligned behavior.

Finally, mastering incentive clarity requires a focus on predictable human behavior. People respond reliably to what they understand, can measure, and see rewarded. Overly complex, opaque, or nuanced incentives undermine this predictability, producing unintended consequences. Leaders, policymakers, educators, and innovators can design more effective systems by simplifying, clarifying, and making incentives transparent. Predictable human behavior ensures that clear rewards are pursued consistently and ethically. Incentive-aware simplicity transforms abstract goals into measurable, actionable outcomes. Clarity strengthens alignment, trust, and sustainable success across all domains.

PART VII — INCENTIVES FOR A SUSTAINABLE FUTURE

Chapter .31

Environmental Collapse Is an Incentive Problem First

Ecological destruction persists because exploitation remains more profitable than preservation.

Environmental crises are rarely caused by ignorance or lack of intention; they are the predictable result of incentive structures that reward short-term exploitation over long-term stewardship. Individuals, corporations, and governments respond rationally to the rewards and penalties they face, making destructive behavior predictable when preservation is less profitable or recognized. Fossil fuel use, deforestation, overfishing, and pollution are often economically incentivized, despite widespread knowledge of their long-term harm. By realigning incentives so that sustainable actions are more rewarding than exploitative ones, human behavior can shift predictably toward ecological preservation. Incentive-aware design transforms environmental responsibility from an ethical aspiration into a rational choice. Understanding this principle is crucial for business leaders, policymakers, and communities seeking to address ecological collapse.

Corporate behavior illustrates the centrality of incentives in environmental outcomes. Businesses respond predictably to cost structures, profit potential, and regulatory rewards or penalties. Companies often choose environmentally harmful practices because they are cheaper, faster, or more profitable in the short term. Conversely, when regulations, subsidies, or market rewards favor sustainable practices—such as renewable energy adoption, carbon credits, or circular economy initiatives—businesses adjust behavior predictably. Aligning corporate incentives with environmental outcomes ensures that economic interests support ecological stewardship. Incentive-aware strategies turn environmental responsibility into a competitive advantage rather than a compliance burden. Businesses naturally follow the rewards presented to them, making incentive design the most effective lever for sustainability.

Government and policy systems face similar challenges. Regulations often fail when the penalties for ecological harm are weak, delayed, or poorly enforced, while short-term economic gains remain strong. Citizens, corporations, and bureaucrats respond predictably to these incentives, exploiting loopholes or prioritizing immediate gain over long-term preservation. Policies that make sustainable behavior more profitable—through taxes, subsidies, or market mechanisms—produce predictable environmental improvement. Multi-level governance, public accountability, and transparent enforcement further amplify positive behavior. Incentive-aware policy design ensures that environmental protection is not optional but economically and socially rational. Making sustainable choices the most rewarding option transforms predictable exploitation into preservation.

Historical examples demonstrate the consequences of misaligned incentives for the environment. Civilizations that exploited forests, water, and soil without accounting for long-term consequences suffered resource depletion, famine, or collapse. Companies and industries that ignored sustainability due to short-term profit motives degraded ecosystems, often with predictable social and economic consequences. Societies that incorporated incentive structures—such as property rights, resource quotas, or economic rewards for stewardship—produced more sustainable outcomes. Predictable human responses to incentives show that ecological collapse is rarely the result of negligence, but rather a misalignment between behavior and reward. Incentive-aware systems can reverse historical patterns of environmental degradation by making preservation profitable and natural.

Personal and community behavior also responds to incentive alignment in environmental contexts. Individuals act predictably when recycling, conservation, energy efficiency, or sustainable consumption is rewarded or recognized. Communities that implement visible, tangible incentives—such as rebates, recognition programs, or community rewards—experience higher engagement in sustainable practices. Misaligned incentives, such as subsidies for polluting activities or lack of recognition for conservation, produce predictable environmental harm. By consciously designing personal, social, and economic incentives, leaders can guide behavior toward preservation rather than exploitation. Predictable human behavior ensures that rewards determine ecological outcomes. Incentive-aware design converts environmental responsibility from moral obligation into rational, actionable choice.

Financial and market mechanisms further highlight the importance of aligning incentives. Investors, banks, and insurance companies respond predictably to the rewards and risks embedded in their environment. Industries that exploit natural resources often do so because the economic incentives outweigh the visible costs. Conversely, systems that integrate sustainability into profitability—such as green bonds, ESG metrics, or carbon pricing—align behavior with ecological outcomes. Predictable human and organizational responses make financial incentive design critical for environmental sustainability. By making preservation economically advantageous, markets guide behavior toward responsible stewardship. Incentive-aware systems ensure that ecological collapse becomes preventable rather than inevitable.

Education and professional development provide another layer of influence. Individuals, from students to professionals, respond predictably when environmental knowledge is coupled with actionable rewards. Sustainability programs, certifications, and recognition for environmentally conscious behavior create incentives that drive predictable, constructive action. Misaligned incentives, such as grading or promotion systems that reward output without consideration of environmental impact, foster destructive behavior. Designing educational systems that reward sustainable practices embeds responsible behavior at an early stage. Incentive-aware learning ensures that ecological consciousness translates into real-world action. Predictable behavior emerges when understanding and reward structures align with environmental preservation.

Technology and innovation are shaped by incentive structures as well. Renewable energy development, sustainable agriculture, and waste reduction technologies advance when financial, social, and regulatory incentives favor adoption. Conversely, technological exploitation without consequences produces predictable harm, such as pollution, resource depletion, and climate change acceleration. Systems that reward sustainable innovation over destructive efficiency drive predictable behavior toward solutions that protect ecosystems. Incentive-aware design aligns technological progress with environmental objectives. Predictable responses to incentives ensure that innovation produces positive impact rather than ecological degradation. Properly structured rewards make sustainability a rational choice across all levels of society.

Finally, mastering environmental stewardship requires recognizing the centrality of incentives. Individuals, organizations, and governments act predictably in response to what is rewarded. Misaligned incentives produce predictable ecological harm, while well-designed structures encourage preservation and sustainable behavior. Leaders, educators, and policymakers must align financial, social, and regulatory rewards to ensure that responsible action is also advantageous. Incentive-aware systems convert ecological preservation from ethical aspiration to predictable, rational behavior. When preservation becomes more rewarding than exploitation, human behavior follows predictably, creating resilient ecosystems and sustainable futures. Aligning incentives is the first and most critical step in preventing environmental collapse.

Chapter .32

Health Systems Incentivize Treatment Over Prevention

Healthcare outcomes improve when incentives reward wellness rather than illness.

Modern health systems often prioritize treatment of disease over prevention, reflecting predictable human responses to incentive structures. Hospitals, clinics, and providers receive compensation for procedures, diagnostics, and interventions rather than for keeping patients healthy. Individuals, likewise, respond to these structures by seeking care reactively instead of proactively managing their health. Misaligned incentives encourage reactive, costly, and often less effective healthcare practices. By realigning incentives to reward prevention, wellness, and early intervention, predictable improvements in public health can occur. Understanding and adjusting these incentive dynamics is crucial for healthcare providers, policymakers, and individuals seeking better outcomes.

Corporate health systems provide clear examples of the problem and potential solutions. Hospitals and insurance companies generate revenue from treatments, surgeries, and chronic care management, while preventive programs such as lifestyle counseling or wellness initiatives are often undervalued. Employees and patients respond predictably to what is financially rewarded, prioritizing treatment over prevention. By incentivizing wellness programs, preventive screenings, and early interventions through subsidies, coverage, or performance-based rewards, organizations can shift behavior toward healthier outcomes. Predictable human behavior ensures that reward structures drive choices, whether at the organizational or individual level. Aligning incentives with prevention reduces costs, improves health outcomes, and increases long-term efficiency. Incentive-aware design transforms healthcare from a reactive system into a proactive, sustainable one.

Government and policy frameworks are similarly affected. National healthcare programs, public health initiatives, and regulations often emphasize treatment metrics rather than preventive outcomes. Physicians, clinics, and citizens respond predictably to the incentives presented, resulting in costly chronic care and episodic treatment. Policies that reward prevention—such as immunization programs, early screenings, and lifestyle interventions—align personal, provider, and societal interests. Predictable human behavior ensures that these incentives improve compliance, engagement, and health outcomes. Incentive-aware policy design transforms healthcare systems into proactive, preventive structures. Making wellness more rewarding than illness ensures sustainable, measurable improvements in population health.

Historical examples reveal the predictable consequences of misaligned health incentives. Societies that neglected prevention in favor of reactive care often faced epidemics, high mortality, and unsustainable healthcare costs. Hospitals and clinics responded to financial reward structures, prioritizing treatment over public health interventions. Conversely, communities that invested in preventive programs, sanitation, and public health education experienced predictable improvements in longevity, quality of life, and economic stability. Incentives, not intention alone, shaped these outcomes. Recognizing predictable responses to reward structures allows policymakers and healthcare leaders to design systems that prioritize health over illness. Incentive-aware frameworks produce sustainable improvements in human wellbeing.

Personal and community behavior also reflects incentive alignment in health. Individuals respond predictably to rewards, recognition, and accessibility, favoring behaviors that are incentivized. When preventive actions such as exercise, healthy eating, and regular check-ups are rewarded or reinforced, engagement increases. Communities that provide visible incentives, public recognition, or social reinforcement for wellness behaviors foster predictable positive outcomes. Misaligned incentives, such as insurance coverage that favors treatment over prevention, discourage proactive health management. By designing personal and community incentives aligned with wellness, predictable improvements in health behavior emerge. Incentive-aware design ensures that individuals prioritize prevention naturally and sustainably.

Financial and organizational considerations highlight the importance of aligning health incentives. Insurance companies, employers, and healthcare providers respond predictably to reward structures that emphasize cost savings and preventive care. Misaligned incentives that compensate only for treatments or interventions produce overuse, inefficiency, and long-term financial strain. By creating reward systems that prioritize early detection, wellness programs, and chronic disease management, predictable positive behavior emerges. Incentive-aware health systems reduce costs, improve outcomes, and foster sustainable practices. Predictable human and organizational behavior makes proper alignment the most powerful lever for transformation. Aligning economic and ethical incentives ensures that prevention becomes the default, not the exception.

Education and professional development for healthcare providers also benefit from incentive clarity. Medical training, performance evaluations, and career advancement often reward procedural skill or acute treatment rather than preventive practice. Predictable responses to these incentives influence the focus and behavior of healthcare professionals. By aligning training and professional rewards with prevention, public health awareness, and long-term patient outcomes, systems encourage constructive, sustainable practice. Incentive-aware design ensures that professional priorities match societal health goals. Predictable human behavior demonstrates that clear, aligned rewards foster wellness-focused culture. Education systems that reward prevention transform healthcare outcomes across generations.

Technology and innovation illustrate similar patterns. Health monitoring apps, telemedicine platforms, and predictive analytics are only effective when incentives encourage proactive engagement and preventive behavior. Users respond predictably to reward structures, and misaligned incentives—such as app designs focused on treatment reminders rather than wellness engagement—limit effectiveness. Platforms that reinforce preventive habits, reward healthy behaviors, and provide immediate feedback align user action with long-term health goals. Incentive-aware technology transforms data and tools into actionable drivers of wellness. Predictable responses to incentives ensure that innovation supports proactive, preventive outcomes. Properly designed systems make prevention the natural, rewarding choice.

Finally, mastering prevention in healthcare requires understanding predictable human and organizational behavior. Individuals, providers, and policymakers act in response to incentives, making alignment critical for sustainable improvement. Misaligned incentives produce predictable overemphasis on treatment and underinvestment in wellness. By designing financial, regulatory, educational, and social incentives that reward prevention, predictable improvements in health outcomes emerge. Incentive-aware design transforms healthcare into a system where wellness is rewarded, disease is minimized, and long-term outcomes are optimized. When prevention becomes the most rewarding choice, human behavior follows predictably, producing healthier, more sustainable societies.

Chapter .33

Education Improves When Learning Beats Credentialing

Students thrive when incentives value mastery over test performance.

Modern education often emphasizes credentials, grades, and rankings over genuine learning, reflecting predictable responses to incentive structures. Students, teachers, and institutions act in ways that maximize what is rewarded, prioritizing test scores, diplomas, or certifications rather than deep understanding. Misaligned incentives produce surface-level engagement, rote memorization, and shallow comprehension. By designing systems that reward mastery, problem-solving, and critical thinking, predictable behaviors shift toward meaningful learning. Incentive-aware education transforms the focus from earning credentials to acquiring knowledge and skills. Understanding this principle is essential for educators, policymakers, and leaders seeking to cultivate true expertise.

Corporate learning programs provide clear examples of the principle. Employees often complete mandatory courses or certifications to satisfy HR requirements rather than acquire actionable skills. Individuals respond predictably to the incentives presented, emphasizing completion and credentials over comprehension. When professional development programs reward demonstrated ability, project success, or skill application, behavior naturally shifts toward mastery. Incentive-aware design ensures that learning becomes practical, relevant, and impactful. Organizations that value competence over certification achieve higher performance, innovation, and engagement. Aligning reward structures with real-world outcomes transforms education into a tool for growth rather than a bureaucratic obligation.

Government and policy systems similarly shape educational outcomes. Public funding, standardized testing, and institutional rankings often incentivize surface-level achievement over deep understanding. Schools, teachers, and administrators respond predictably, focusing on measurable metrics rather than genuine skill development. Policies that reward innovation in teaching, competency-based outcomes, and applied learning encourage constructive behavior. Incentive-aware design ensures that both educators and students prioritize mastery over mere certification. Predictable human behavior demonstrates that aligning incentives with learning goals improves educational outcomes consistently. Systems that value learning over credentials cultivate critical thinking, creativity, and lifelong competence.

Historical examples illustrate the consequences of misaligned educational incentives. Societies that prioritized diplomas or formal titles over practical knowledge often produced graduates with impressive credentials but limited skills. Conversely, systems emphasizing mastery, apprenticeship, or hands-on problem-solving produced predictable improvements in productivity, innovation, and social mobility. Individuals respond rationally to the rewards presented, making credential-focused systems predictable drivers of surface-level achievement. Incentive-aware reform allows education to produce competent, capable individuals rather than mere title holders. Aligning incentives with learning ensures that knowledge, creativity, and problem-solving are cultivated systematically. History demonstrates that mastery-driven systems produce durable societal benefits.

Personal and community behavior also reflects the effects of incentives in education. Students focus on what is rewarded, whether that is test performance, grades, or practical problem-solving. Communities, parents, and peers reinforce these behaviors through recognition, support, or pressure. Misaligned incentives, such as excessive focus on standardized assessments, create predictable disengagement, stress, and superficial learning. By emphasizing mastery, skill application, and problem-solving as the primary rewards, individuals are guided toward meaningful educational outcomes. Incentive-aware design at the personal and community level ensures that learning becomes an end in itself, not merely a credential. Predictable behavior emerges when reward structures reflect the values of understanding, competence, and lifelong growth.

Financial and organizational considerations further highlight the principle. Employers, investors, and professional networks respond predictably to the incentives presented by educational attainment. Degrees, certifications, and rankings often dominate hiring and promotion decisions, encouraging individuals to focus on credentials rather than competence. By rewarding demonstrated skill, problem-solving, and applied knowledge, organizations create predictable alignment between education and real-world performance. Incentive-aware systems in workforce development ensure that talent pipelines emphasize mastery over formal recognition. Predictable responses to rewards make incentive alignment a powerful driver of capability, innovation, and productivity. Education becomes a tool for creating real value rather than merely signaling achievement.

Technology and learning platforms also illustrate the impact of incentives. Online courses, digital learning tools, and gamified education systems often reward completion, streaks, or point accumulation instead of mastery or understanding. Users respond predictably to the metrics emphasized by the system, producing engagement without competence. Platforms that incentivize skill application, critical thinking, and measurable improvement encourage constructive learning behavior. Incentive-aware design transforms technology into a means of fostering deep understanding rather than superficial achievement. Predictable behavior ensures that learners internalize knowledge and can apply it effectively. Aligning incentives with mastery ensures that education produces capable, adaptable, and skilled individuals.

Finally, mastering education as a system requires aligning incentives with learning rather than credentials. Students, educators, and institutions respond predictably to what is rewarded, making behavior the primary lever for improvement. Misaligned incentives encourage superficial engagement, stress, and rote memorization, while mastery-focused rewards produce enduring competence. By designing educational systems that recognize skill, understanding, and problem-solving, predictable behavior shifts toward genuine learning. Incentive-aware frameworks transform credentials from the goal into a byproduct of competence. When learning is more rewarding than credentialing, human behavior follows predictably, producing a society of skilled, capable, and adaptable individuals. Aligning incentives with mastery ensures education achieves its intended purpose: developing understanding and competence.

Chapter .34

Inequality Grows When Incentives Compound Advantage

Fair systems reduce runaway benefits that lock inequality in place.

Inequality is often a predictable result of incentive structures that reward the already advantaged more than those with less. Wealth, opportunity, and influence tend to accumulate when systems disproportionately benefit those who already have resources, education, or social capital. Individuals respond rationally to these structures, making behavior predictable: the advantaged capitalize further, while the disadvantaged struggle to gain traction. Misaligned incentives create cycles of compounded advantage, producing systemic inequality that is difficult to reverse. By designing incentives that level the playing field and reward contribution over inherited privilege, society can reduce entrenched disparities. Incentive-aware design ensures that opportunity and reward are distributed in ways that promote fairness and sustainable prosperity.

Corporate systems demonstrate the impact of compounding advantage. Executives, investors, and high-performing employees often receive escalating bonuses, stock options, and privileges that grow disproportionately relative to others in the organization. Employees respond predictably to these reward structures, with high earners leveraging advantages to further their position and resources. Conversely, entry-level workers, lacking access to comparable opportunities, see minimal upward mobility. By designing incentive systems that reward collaboration, mentorship, and equitable contribution, organizations can reduce predictable inequality. Incentive-aware compensation structures ensure that growth and rewards are broadly shared while still incentivizing performance. Aligning individual and collective incentives prevents runaway disparities that undermine morale and organizational cohesion.

Government policies and social systems are equally influenced by incentive structures. Tax codes, social benefits, and access to education or healthcare often create conditions where the wealthy gain more rapidly than those with fewer resources. Citizens, businesses, and policymakers respond predictably to these incentives, producing cycles of compounded advantage. Policies that reduce these imbalances—such as progressive taxation, targeted subsidies, and broad access to education—align behavior with social equity. Predictable responses to incentives make structural inequality solvable if systems are consciously designed to reward contribution and opportunity rather than mere existing advantage. Incentive-aware governance ensures fairness, mobility, and sustainable economic growth. Misaligned incentives predictably exacerbate inequality, while aligned incentives foster a more just society.

Historical examples demonstrate the consequences of compounded advantage. Aristocracies, guilds, and monopolistic enterprises accumulated disproportionate wealth and influence over generations, limiting opportunity for others. Systems that rewarded inheritance, position, or social standing created predictable entrenchment of privilege. Conversely, societies that implemented mechanisms such as land redistribution, progressive education, or meritocratic structures produced more balanced outcomes. Human behavior responds predictably to reward structures, reinforcing the importance of incentive design. Incentive-aware frameworks ensure that advantages are not self-perpetuating but instead reward effort, contribution, and equitable participation. Addressing compounded advantage requires deliberate alignment of incentives with fairness and opportunity.

Personal and community behavior also illustrates this principle. Individuals respond predictably to systems that reward existing privilege or wealth accumulation, reinforcing inequality in neighborhoods, social networks, and families. Communities that emphasize merit, collaboration, and shared reward structures foster predictable engagement and upward mobility. Misaligned incentives, such as favoritism, nepotism, or unbalanced access to opportunities, produce predictable stagnation and inequity. By consciously designing personal, educational, and social reward structures to mitigate compounding advantages, communities can encourage fairer outcomes. Incentive-aware behavior ensures that effort, talent, and contribution drive success rather than inherited privilege. Aligning rewards with merit and shared opportunity transforms predictable behavior into a force for equitable growth.

Financial and market systems highlight the importance of addressing compounded advantage. Investors, banks, and corporations naturally accumulate resources when early success or initial capital is disproportionately rewarded. Predictable responses to these incentives reinforce systemic wealth concentration. By creating structures that reward innovation, contribution, and broad participation rather than solely initial capital, markets can reduce inequality. Incentive-aware design ensures that wealth creation is accessible, distributed, and sustainable. Predictable human and organizational behavior makes alignment essential for fairness, economic stability, and social cohesion. Systems that consciously prevent runaway advantage create predictable pathways for broad prosperity.

Education and professional development also demonstrate the power of incentives in addressing inequality. Access to advanced learning, mentorship, and skill-building opportunities often compounds advantage for already privileged students. Predictable behavior reinforces disparities when incentives favor credential accumulation, elite institutions, or selective opportunities. By designing equitable incentives—such as scholarships, mentorship programs, and performance-based recognition—education systems can reduce compounding advantages. Incentive-aware design ensures that talent and effort are rewarded fairly, creating predictable pathways for upward mobility. Predictable responses to aligned incentives ensure that educational success is based on contribution and mastery rather than preexisting advantage. Equity-focused design transforms education into a tool for social mobility rather than entrenchment.

Technology and innovation reveal similar patterns. Platforms, networks, and digital systems often amplify the advantages of early adopters, influencers, or resource-rich participants. Users respond predictably to the reward structures embedded in these systems, leading to compounding success for the advantaged. By intentionally designing incentives that broaden participation, reward contribution, and provide equal access to tools, platforms can reduce predictable inequality. Incentive-aware design ensures that technological adoption benefits the many rather than just the already advantaged. Predictable behavior underscores the importance of aligning incentives with fairness and equitable opportunity. Technology becomes a tool for inclusion rather than concentration when reward structures are intentionally designed.

Finally, mastering the reduction of inequality requires understanding predictable human behavior and systemic dynamics. Individuals, organizations, and societies act in response to incentives, making compounding advantage predictable without intervention. Misaligned structures produce entrenched disparities, while carefully designed incentives promote fairness, opportunity, and mobility. By aligning rewards with contribution, effort, and equitable participation, predictable behavior shifts toward shared prosperity. Incentive-aware systems reduce inequality, foster stability, and empower communities to thrive. When incentives counteract compounding advantage, human behavior naturally promotes fairness, growth, and sustainable social development. Aligning individual gain with collective opportunity is essential for building a just and resilient society.

Chapter .35

Resilient Societies Reward Contribution, Not Extraction

Stability emerges when systems incentivize value creation over value capture.

Resilient societies are built on incentive structures that reward individuals and organizations for contributing value rather than extracting it from others. When systems prioritize short-term gain, rent-seeking, or exploitation, predictable behaviors emerge that erode trust, collaboration, and long-term stability. Individuals respond rationally to what is rewarded, meaning extraction-based incentives perpetuate cycles of inequality, corruption, and inefficiency. Conversely, aligning incentives with contribution, innovation, and shared benefit produces predictable cooperation and sustainable growth. Incentive-aware design strengthens communities, economies, and institutions by ensuring that behavior is aligned with societal well-being. Understanding this principle is essential for leaders, policymakers, and citizens striving to create resilient systems.

Corporate and organizational examples illustrate this principle clearly. Companies that reward employees for innovation, collaboration, and client value creation outperform those that incentivize short-term sales, manipulation, or internal competition. Predictable human behavior ensures that when contribution is rewarded, employees invest time, energy, and creativity into work that benefits the organization and its stakeholders. Extraction-focused rewards, such as aggressive cost-cutting at the expense of colleagues or clients, undermine morale and long-term performance. Incentive-aware corporate design fosters sustainable growth by making contribution the most rational path to personal and organizational success. Aligning individual gain with collective value produces predictable, positive outcomes. Systems that reward creation over extraction cultivate loyalty, trust, and enduring competitive advantage.

Government and policy systems demonstrate the broader societal implications of incentives. Citizens, public officials, and institutions respond predictably to reward structures, meaning policies that favor rent-seeking, subsidies for extraction, or opportunistic behavior undermine social cohesion. Conversely, policies that reward civic contribution, innovation, and public service align personal incentives with societal good. Incentive-aware governance produces predictable engagement, compliance, and social trust. Social programs, taxation, and regulatory structures that incentivize contribution over exploitation strengthen societal resilience. Misaligned incentives encourage predictable behavior that erodes stability, while aligned incentives foster shared prosperity. Building resilient societies requires designing policies that make constructive behavior more rewarding than exploitation.

Historical examples reinforce the importance of rewarding contribution. Civilizations that incentivized value creation—through trade, innovation, and public service—tended to flourish, while societies that allowed unchecked extraction often experienced decline, corruption, and collapse. Human behavior responds predictably to reward structures, creating systems where extraction produces short-term gain but long-term instability. Societies that aligned personal and collective incentives with contribution produced lasting wealth, cultural advancement, and institutional resilience. Incentive-aware systems recognize that predictable behavior can either build or destroy societal foundations. Aligning rewards with contribution ensures that individual and collective actions reinforce stability, prosperity, and trust. History demonstrates that extraction-focused systems produce predictable societal fragility.

Personal and community behavior also reflects the impact of incentive alignment. Individuals naturally invest effort, time, and resources in ways that are rewarded, whether through recognition, financial gain, or social influence. Communities that recognize and reinforce constructive contribution foster predictable cooperation, participation, and social capital. Misaligned incentives, which reward exploitation or opportunism, produce predictable disengagement, conflict, and distrust. By designing personal, social, and community incentives to reward value creation, leaders cultivate resilient networks and collaborative environments. Incentive-aware behavior ensures that individuals act in ways that strengthen social bonds and collective well-being. Aligning personal incentives with communal benefit transforms predictable behavior into sustainable contribution.

Financial and market systems further illustrate the importance of rewarding contribution. Investors, entrepreneurs, and organizations respond predictably to reward structures, prioritizing profit over impact when incentives favor extraction. Systems that incentivize value creation—such as fair investment structures, equitable profit-sharing, or social enterprise metrics—align individual gain with societal benefit. Predictable human and organizational behavior ensures that contribution-focused rewards generate innovation, growth, and resilience. Misaligned incentives create systemic fragility, inequality, and exploitation, eroding long-term stability. Incentive-aware design in financial systems transforms economic activity from a zero-sum game into a value-creating engine. Rewarding contribution over extraction produces predictable prosperity for both individuals and society.

Education and professional development also benefit from aligning incentives with contribution. Students, trainees, and professionals respond predictably to rewards that recognize applied skill, mentorship, and societal benefit. Credential-focused or competition-driven incentives often foster extraction-oriented behaviors, such as knowledge hoarding or opportunistic advancement. By designing educational systems that reward contribution, collaboration, and applied learning, predictable positive behavior emerges. Incentive-aware education ensures that individuals develop skills and habits that enhance communities, organizations, and society. Aligning rewards with contribution transforms predictable personal development into societal resilience. Systems that recognize and reinforce value creation cultivate capable, responsible, and engaged citizens.

Technology and innovation provide further evidence of the principle. Platforms, algorithms, and digital systems respond predictably to incentives, rewarding behaviors that the system amplifies. Systems that favor extraction—such as clickbait monetization, misinformation, or exploitative practices—produce predictable social and economic harm. Conversely, platforms that incentivize value creation, knowledge sharing, and constructive engagement generate positive, lasting outcomes. Incentive-aware design ensures that technology amplifies contribution rather than exploitation. Predictable human responses to incentives allow systems to reinforce innovation, collaboration, and community benefit. Aligning rewards with contribution makes technological systems resilient, ethical, and impactful.

Finally, mastering resilient societal design requires recognizing the central role of incentives. Individuals, organizations, and governments act predictably in response to what is rewarded. Misaligned incentives encourage extraction, short-termism, and instability, while systems that reward contribution foster cooperation, trust, and sustainability. By aligning personal, institutional, and systemic incentives with value creation, predictable behaviors produce resilient, thriving societies. Incentive-aware systems convert self-interest into a force for collective good, making ethical and constructive action the rational choice. Rewarding contribution over extraction ensures that human behavior reinforces stability, prosperity, and shared success. Aligning incentives with value creation is the foundation of resilient, enduring societies.

Part VIII — Becoming an Incentive Architect

Chapter .36

You Are Already Designing Incentives Every Day

Personal, professional, and social choices constantly shape incentive structures.

Every action you take influences the behavior of others, whether intentionally or not, creating predictable incentive effects. From the way you communicate expectations to how you reward effort or recognize achievement, people respond to the incentives you create. Families, workplaces, and communities all operate on implicit and explicit reward structures, meaning you are already a designer of incentives. Ignoring this reality leaves outcomes to chance, often producing predictable misalignment or undesired behavior. By consciously understanding and shaping the incentives you influence, you can guide behavior toward constructive, ethical, and productive outcomes. Incentive-aware individuals leverage this understanding to transform daily interactions into predictable pathways for success.

Corporate and professional environments demonstrate the power of everyday incentives. Managers, team leaders, and executives constantly influence behavior through recognition, task assignment, feedback, and promotion. Employees respond predictably to the incentives embedded in organizational culture, whether formal or informal. Subtle actions, such as public acknowledgment or prioritization of certain behaviors, create reinforcement loops that shape long-term patterns. Incentive-aware leaders recognize that every decision and communication sets a precedent, producing predictable behaviors throughout the team or organization. By intentionally designing these everyday incentives, leaders can cultivate engagement, innovation, and collaboration. Understanding the influence of daily interactions transforms management from reactive supervision to proactive behavioral design.

Government, policy, and social systems function similarly at the individual level. Citizens, colleagues, and institutions respond predictably to the behaviors we reward or discourage in our interactions, communities, and networks. Even small acts, such as voting for policies, advocating for fairness, or mentoring others, create incentives that shape the choices of others. Misaligned or unconscious incentives perpetuate negative behavior, while conscious alignment fosters constructive action. Individuals who recognize their influence on incentive structures can amplify positive social and civic outcomes. Incentive-aware behavior at the personal level contributes to predictable improvements in community and societal function. By understanding your role in shaping incentives, everyday decisions become a powerful tool for systemic impact.

Historical examples illustrate the compounding effects of everyday incentive design. Leaders, educators, and community figures who consciously aligned small rewards, expectations, and recognition with desired behaviors produced predictable long-term societal benefits. Conversely, unchecked negative reinforcement, favoritism, or misaligned recognition fostered predictable dysfunction, exploitation, or stagnation. Human behavior responds reliably to incentives, making the cumulative effect of daily actions significant. Incentive-aware individuals recognize that influence is not limited to formal authority but is embedded in every interaction. Small choices, when intentionally aligned with desired outcomes, produce predictable and lasting effects. Understanding this principle enables individuals to intentionally shape systems at micro and macro scales.

Personal and community behavior also responds predictably to everyday incentives. Families, neighbors, and social groups establish reward structures that influence behavior, such as praise for helpfulness, accountability for commitments, or recognition for innovation. Misaligned or inconsistent reinforcement produces predictable disengagement, conflict, or harmful behavior. By consciously designing incentives at the micro level—through encouragement, expectation setting, and acknowledgment—predictable alignment with values and goals emerges. Incentive-aware individuals leverage these small, daily decisions to cultivate communities that reward constructive behavior and discourage destructive actions. Predictable human responses demonstrate that intentional reinforcement shapes culture, norms, and productivity. Every interaction, conversation, and reward choice contributes to the broader system of incentives influencing behavior.

Financial and organizational behavior illustrates similar patterns. Employees, partners, and clients respond predictably to incentives embedded in communication, recognition, and resource allocation. Subtle decisions, such as which projects receive attention, how performance is acknowledged, or which behaviors are tolerated, reinforce patterns of engagement, collaboration, and ethical conduct. Misaligned or opaque daily incentives produce predictable inefficiency, low morale, or unethical behavior. Incentive-aware leaders understand that even small, consistent actions set precedent and shape behavior over time. By consciously designing daily incentives, organizations achieve predictable alignment between individual behavior and strategic objectives. Predictable human responses to reinforcement demonstrate that everyday incentive design is a continuous, high-impact activity.

Education and professional development provide additional applications. Teachers, mentors, and coaches influence behavior predictably through the incentives they create in classrooms and training environments. Recognition, feedback, challenge, and opportunity reinforce certain behaviors, while lack of attention or misaligned priorities produces predictable disengagement. By intentionally aligning these incentives with mastery, collaboration, and contribution, educators cultivate sustained, constructive engagement. Incentive-aware design transforms micro-level interactions into predictable behavioral patterns that support growth, learning, and ethical development. Predictable human behavior ensures that small, consistent reinforcements produce cumulative positive outcomes. Understanding your role in daily incentive design allows individuals to influence learning and development systematically.

Technology and innovation also respond to everyday incentive structures. Platforms, social networks, and collaborative tools amplify behavior based on reinforcement mechanisms embedded in usage, attention, or feedback loops. Users respond predictably to these structures, producing desired or harmful patterns of engagement. By consciously designing digital incentives—through feedback, recognition, or gamification—predictable, constructive behavior emerges. Incentive-aware creators shape digital environments that reward contribution, collaboration, and ethical use. Small design choices produce predictable cascading effects at scale. Understanding and leveraging everyday incentive design in technology magnifies the impact of intentional human behavior.

Finally, mastering everyday incentive design requires recognizing your constant influence on human behavior. Individuals, leaders, and communities act predictably in response to the rewards, expectations, and recognition embedded in daily interactions. Misaligned or unconscious incentives produce predictable misbehavior, inefficiency, or disengagement, while conscious alignment fosters constructive, ethical, and productive action. By intentionally designing the incentives present in your words, choices, and systems, predictable positive outcomes emerge. Incentive-aware individuals transform ordinary interactions into powerful tools for long-term success, ethical alignment, and systemic improvement. Every decision you make, every recognition you give, and every behavior you reward contributes to the predictable shaping of human systems. Understanding your role as an incentive designer turns daily life into a deliberate, high-impact opportunity.

Chapter .37

Leadership Is the Art of Incentive Alignment

Effective leaders focus less on control and more on reward design to guide predictable, constructive behavior.

Leadership is less about commanding compliance and more about shaping behavior through strategically aligned incentives. Leaders influence teams, organizations, and communities by creating systems where the most rewarded behaviors are those that align with collective goals. Human behavior responds predictably to incentives, making alignment the most effective tool for driving performance, collaboration, and ethical action. Misaligned incentives, even with the best intentions, produce unintended outcomes, frustration, and inefficiency. By consciously designing rewards, recognition, and consequences, leaders guide predictable behavior toward desired outcomes. Incentive-aware leadership transforms management from reactive control into proactive behavioral architecture.

Corporate environments demonstrate the power of incentive-aligned leadership. Executives and managers who prioritize compensation, recognition, and growth opportunities that align individual and organizational objectives see predictable improvements in productivity and engagement. Employees respond to structures where effort, creativity, and collaboration are rewarded while misalignment or opportunism is discouraged. Misaligned leadership—rewarding speed over quality, competition over teamwork, or appearance over substance—produces predictable disengagement, errors, and conflict. By aligning incentives across departments, career tracks, and team goals, leaders create predictable patterns of constructive behavior. Incentive-aware design ensures that employees pursue organizational objectives naturally and sustainably. Leadership becomes a lever for systemic performance rather than short-term control.

Government and policy leaders face similar challenges in aligning incentives to achieve societal goals. Citizens, bureaucrats, and institutions respond predictably to what is rewarded or penalized. Policies or programs that reward compliance rather than outcomes, short-term gains rather than long-term stability, or individual advancement over public service produce predictable inefficiency or exploitation. Leaders who align incentives with desired societal behavior—through taxation, subsidies, recognition, or regulation—guide predictable, constructive outcomes. Incentive-aware leadership at the policy level ensures that human behavior naturally supports societal goals. Aligning rewards with contribution, innovation, and collaboration transforms governance into a tool for predictable improvement. Leadership, in this sense, is less about directives and more about structuring rewards to shape behavior.

Historical examples highlight the impact of incentive-aligned leadership. Leaders who understood and leveraged incentives—rewarding loyalty, contribution, innovation, or public service—produced predictable stability and prosperity. Conversely, rulers and managers who misaligned incentives, rewarding favoritism, exploitation, or short-term gain, generated predictable dysfunction, corruption, and decline. Human behavior responds systematically to incentives, so leadership effectiveness depends on careful reward design. Incentive-aware leaders recognize that their influence extends beyond orders to the structures they create, producing predictable patterns of behavior across populations. Strategic alignment of incentives becomes the defining feature of resilient, successful leadership. Leaders who master incentive architecture shape outcomes without relying on coercion or control.

Personal and community leadership reflects similar dynamics. Individuals who influence families, volunteer groups, or social networks shape behavior predictably through the incentives they set. Recognition, access to resources, responsibility, and social validation are all levers that guide behavior. Misaligned incentives, such as favoritism or inconsistent reinforcement, produce predictable disengagement, conflict, or unethical action. By consciously aligning incentives with desired behaviors—support, contribution, learning, or collaboration—leaders cultivate predictable engagement and constructive action. Incentive-aware leadership transforms everyday interactions into systemic tools for ethical, cooperative, and high-performing communities. Predictable human responses ensure that aligned incentives create long-lasting, positive impact in both personal and professional contexts.

Financial and organizational systems further illustrate the importance of incentive-aligned leadership. Executives, investors, and employees respond predictably to compensation, promotion, and recognition structures. Misalignment, such as rewarding revenue growth at the expense of ethics, collaboration, or sustainability, produces predictable misbehavior, risk-taking, and inefficiency. By designing incentive systems that balance individual reward with organizational and societal goals, leaders produce predictable alignment of effort and outcome. Incentive-aware leadership ensures that capital, authority, and opportunity reinforce contribution, innovation, and ethical behavior. Predictable human behavior guarantees that well-aligned incentives create sustainable growth and trust. Leadership is not simply about directing action—it is about shaping the reward landscape so that predictable behavior supports shared goals.

Education and professional development provide additional examples of incentive-aligned leadership. Educators, mentors, and managers influence behavior predictably through recognition, feedback, and structured opportunities. Misaligned incentives—emphasizing grades, certification, or appearance over mastery, contribution, or growth—produce predictable disengagement or superficial achievement. By aligning rewards with learning, skill application, collaboration, and innovation, leaders in educational and professional contexts guide predictable behavior toward mastery and competence. Incentive-aware leadership ensures that individuals develop the habits, skills, and behaviors necessary for personal and organizational success. Predictable responses to aligned rewards create cultures of continuous improvement, accountability, and contribution. Leaders who master incentive design produce environments where achievement, ethical action, and innovation are self-reinforcing.

Technology and innovation illustrate the role of incentive-aligned leadership at scale. Platforms, software, and collaborative systems respond predictably to incentives embedded in rules, feedback, and reward mechanisms. Misaligned incentives, such as rewarding clickbait, competition, or exploitation, produce predictable negative behavior across vast networks. Leaders who design systems that reward constructive engagement, contribution, and collaboration align human behavior with long-term goals. Incentive-aware leadership ensures that digital ecosystems produce positive, sustainable outcomes. Predictable human behavior in response to reward structures magnifies the impact of well-aligned incentives at scale. Leadership, whether in technology or society, becomes a force for predictable, constructive action when rewards and contributions are carefully designed.

Finally, mastering leadership as the art of incentive alignment requires understanding predictable human behavior. People respond reliably to rewards, recognition, and reinforcement, making alignment the most powerful tool for shaping outcomes. Misaligned incentives produce predictable dysfunction, while aligned incentives produce engagement, collaboration, and ethical behavior. By intentionally structuring rewards and consequences, leaders guide behavior toward desired goals without relying solely on authority or coercion. Incentive-aware leadership transforms influence into a predictable, constructive, and sustainable force. Aligning incentives with desired outcomes is the defining skill of effective leaders across business, policy, and community contexts.

Predictable human behavior, guided by well-designed incentives, ensures that leadership produces lasting, positive impact.

CHAPTER .38

ETHICAL SYSTEMS REQUIRE MORAL INCENTIVES

Values must be reinforced through tangible consequences to endure in predictable human behavior.

Ethical behavior is rarely sustained by intention alone; predictable human behavior responds to the incentives embedded in the environment. Individuals, organizations, and societies act according to rewards and consequences, making moral principles fragile without aligned incentives. Systems that fail to reinforce ethical behavior with tangible rewards or penalties often produce predictable misconduct, corruption, or negligence. By designing incentives that encourage ethical decision-making and discourage wrongdoing, predictable alignment between values and actions emerges. Incentive-aware systems embed morality into human behavior, ensuring that ethical principles are not merely aspirational but consistently practiced. Understanding this dynamic is essential for leaders, policymakers, and individuals seeking durable integrity.

Corporate environments provide clear illustrations of moral incentives in action. Organizations that reward honesty, accountability, and fairness foster predictable ethical behavior among employees. Conversely, cultures that prioritize profit or advancement over ethics incentivize deception, manipulation, and risk-taking at the expense of integrity. By aligning compensation, recognition, and promotion structures with ethical behavior, organizations ensure that doing the right thing is both rational and rewarding. Incentive-aware leadership produces predictable adherence to ethical norms and sustainable corporate culture. Misaligned incentives, even in well-intentioned organizations, produce predictable ethical lapses. Embedding moral incentives transforms ethics from a guideline into a predictable driver of behavior.

Government and policy systems similarly rely on moral incentives to achieve desired outcomes. Citizens, bureaucrats, and public officials respond predictably to systems that reward compliance, transparency, and public service while penalizing corruption, exploitation, or negligence. Policies and institutions that fail to align incentives with ethical conduct produce predictable misconduct, inefficiency, and public distrust. By consciously structuring reward and accountability mechanisms, policymakers ensure predictable adherence to laws, norms, and regulations. Incentive-aware governance fosters civic virtue and societal stability. Misaligned or absent moral incentives erode trust, producing predictable systemic failures. Aligning ethical rewards with human behavior transforms public institutions into predictable engines of integrity.

Historical examples reinforce the importance of moral incentives. Societies, organizations, and institutions that embedded tangible consequences for ethical behavior—through recognition, reward, or accountability—produced predictable patterns of integrity and social cohesion. Conversely, those that failed to reinforce ethical norms faced corruption, exploitation, and decline. Human behavior consistently responds to incentives, demonstrating that ethical systems require alignment between values and reinforcement mechanisms. Incentive-aware design ensures that moral principles are operationalized through predictable consequences rather than abstract ideals. Predictable alignment between reward structures and values strengthens both individual and collective integrity. History confirms that ethical systems endure only when behavior is reliably reinforced.

Personal and community behavior also reflects the necessity of moral incentives. Families, social groups, and local communities influence behavior predictably through reinforcement, recognition, and accountability. Acts of honesty, fairness, and cooperation are more likely to be repeated when consistently rewarded or socially reinforced. Misaligned incentives, such as rewarding opportunism or ignoring misconduct, produce predictable unethical behavior. By intentionally designing personal and community incentive structures that reward ethical behavior and discourage harm, individuals shape predictable patterns of moral action. Incentive-aware behavior fosters trust, cooperation, and sustainable relationships. Predictable responses to moral incentives ensure that ethical behavior becomes habitual and self-reinforcing at every level of society.

Financial and market systems further illustrate the principle. Investors, employees, and executives respond predictably to the reward structures embedded in contracts, compensation, and performance metrics. Systems that fail to reward integrity or penalize exploitation produce predictable misconduct, fraud, or shortsighted risk-taking. By aligning financial incentives with ethical behavior—such as transparency, accountability, and socially responsible practices—predictable compliance and constructive behavior emerge. Incentive-aware financial design ensures that profit and ethics reinforce each other rather than conflict. Predictable human behavior confirms that moral incentives are essential for sustainable economic systems. Aligning reward structures with ethical standards creates markets that consistently support long-term value creation and trust.

Education and professional development also demonstrate the power of moral incentives. Students, trainees, and professionals respond predictably to systems that reward honesty, effort, and collaboration while discouraging plagiarism, shortcuts, or exploitation. Misaligned incentives, such as emphasizing grades over learning or competition over integrity, produce predictable unethical behavior. By designing recognition, feedback, and assessment structures that reinforce ethical action, educators cultivate predictable adherence to moral norms. Incentive-aware educational design ensures that competence, contribution, and integrity are mutually reinforcing. Predictable responses to ethical rewards foster professional and personal growth grounded in values. Aligning educational incentives with moral principles creates individuals who consistently make responsible, constructive choices.

Technology and innovation highlight the need for moral incentives at scale. Platforms, algorithms, and digital systems respond predictably to the reward structures embedded in user experience, moderation, and content promotion. Systems that reward exploitation, deception, or manipulation produce predictable harm and unethical outcomes. Conversely, technology designed to reward transparency, accuracy, and constructive engagement fosters predictable positive behavior. Incentive-aware design ensures that digital tools reinforce ethical action rather than undermining it. Predictable human responses confirm that moral incentives must be embedded in both human and technological systems. Aligning reward structures with ethical outcomes transforms digital spaces into environments that consistently support integrity and social good.

Finally, mastering ethical systems requires recognizing the central role of moral incentives. Individuals, organizations, and societies act predictably in response to the rewards and consequences embedded in their environment. Misaligned or absent moral incentives produce predictable misconduct, disengagement, and harm, while aligned systems foster cooperation, integrity, and sustainable progress. By intentionally designing incentives that reinforce ethical behavior, predictable alignment between values and action emerges. Incentive-aware systems transform abstract morality into operationalized, measurable behavior. Predictable human responses to moral incentives ensure that integrity endures across personal, organizational, and societal contexts. Aligning ethics with tangible consequences is essential for creating systems where doing the right thing is the rational, rewarding choice.

CHAPTER .39

SMALL INCENTIVE CHANGES CAN PRODUCE MASSIVE RESULTS

Minor structural adjustments often outperform sweeping reforms when predictable human behavior responds to well-designed rewards.

Small, carefully designed incentives have the power to produce outsized changes because human behavior is highly sensitive to reward structures. Even minor adjustments—such as recognition, small bonuses, social acknowledgment, or subtle feedback—can alter predictable patterns of action dramatically. Large-scale reforms often fail because they overlook the predictable micro-level responses of individuals to incentives. By focusing on small, actionable changes that align behavior with goals, leaders can achieve significant results efficiently. Incentive-aware design ensures that predictable human behavior works in favor of desired outcomes rather than against them. Understanding the power of small incentives allows for high-impact interventions across business, policy, and personal development contexts.

Corporate and organizational examples illustrate the multiplier effect of small incentive adjustments. Changing performance metrics, providing immediate recognition, or subtly altering the reward structure for teamwork can produce predictable improvements in engagement, collaboration, and productivity. Employees respond predictably when minor adjustments make desired behaviors more rewarding than existing alternatives. Misaligned or ignored incentives, even small ones, produce predictable disengagement or counterproductive behavior.

Incentive-aware managers can leverage micro-adjustments to reshape culture, boost efficiency, and align behavior with strategic goals. Predictable human behavior amplifies the impact of small, well-designed incentives across entire organizations. Even minor adjustments can cascade into transformational results when carefully applied.

Government and policy systems similarly benefit from small incentive interventions. Citizens, bureaucrats, and service providers respond predictably to modest rewards or penalties embedded in programs and regulations. Minor adjustments—such as reducing friction in compliance, providing timely recognition, or aligning small subsidies—produce disproportionately positive outcomes. Large reforms often fail because they overlook predictable responses to micro-level incentives. By focusing on small, targeted changes that align behavior with desired societal outcomes, policymakers can achieve massive results efficiently. Incentive-aware governance leverages predictable human behavior to maximize impact with minimal resources. Minor adjustments can shift civic engagement, compliance, and public service in meaningful, sustainable ways.

Historical examples highlight the outsized impact of small incentive changes. Societies, organizations, and movements that implemented minor adjustments in reward structures often produced predictable, long-term transformations. Small innovations in recognition, access, or responsibility altered human behavior systematically, producing large-scale societal or organizational change. Conversely, large-scale reforms that ignored predictable human responses frequently failed or produced unintended consequences. Incentive-aware design demonstrates that minor, precise adjustments are often more effective than sweeping overhauls. Predictable behavior ensures that small changes can cascade into profound, systemic results. History confirms that thoughtful micro-level incentive design drives disproportionate success over time.

Personal and community behavior also responds predictably to small incentive changes. Families, neighborhoods, and social groups adjust behavior when even minor rewards or recognition are introduced. Acts of encouragement, acknowledgment, or subtle reinforcement produce predictable increases in constructive action. Misaligned incentives or lack of recognition produce predictable disengagement, conflict, or inefficiency. By designing minor adjustments that reward contribution, learning, or collaboration, individuals can achieve significant impact in their communities and networks. Incentive-aware micro-changes leverage predictable behavior to produce exponential benefits over time. Small, intentional interventions consistently generate massive results when applied with understanding of human incentives.

Financial and market systems provide additional illustrations. Investors, employees, and entrepreneurs respond predictably to even minor shifts in reward structures, risk-sharing, or recognition. Slight modifications in performance bonuses, equity incentives, or feedback mechanisms can produce predictable improvements in behavior, innovation, and collaboration. Systems that fail to consider these small, predictable responses often underperform despite large-scale investment or reform. Incentive-aware design leverages micro-level adjustments to align financial behavior with broader organizational and societal goals. Predictable human responses amplify the impact of small, well-calibrated incentives. Minor adjustments, when strategically implemented, often outperform extensive, disruptive interventions.

Education and professional development benefit similarly from small incentive changes. Students, trainees, and employees respond predictably to minor adjustments in recognition, grading, or feedback structures. Small shifts—such as emphasizing mastery over rote performance or rewarding curiosity and contribution—produce outsized engagement and skill development. Misaligned incentives, even subtle ones, produce predictable disengagement or superficial effort. Incentive-aware educators and mentors harness micro-level adjustments to align behavior with learning objectives. Predictable human behavior ensures that minor changes in incentives produce disproportionate improvements in understanding, competence, and performance. Strategic micro-adjustments consistently yield massive educational and professional results.

Technology and innovation highlight the multiplier effect of small incentive changes at scale. Digital platforms, tools, and algorithms respond predictably to minor adjustments in reward systems, feedback loops, and user recognition. Slight modifications can dramatically alter engagement, collaboration, and ethical behavior. Systems that ignore predictable human responses to incentives often produce unintended or destructive outcomes. Incentive-aware design ensures that small changes in technological reward structures produce predictable and positive behavior at scale. Predictable human responses amplify the impact of carefully designed micro-level interventions. Minor incentive adjustments can transform digital environments into powerful engines for engagement, learning, and constructive behavior.

Finally, mastering the power of small incentive changes requires understanding predictable human behavior. Individuals, organizations, and societies respond reliably to rewards and reinforcement, making micro-level adjustments a potent lever for systemic impact. Misaligned or ignored incentives, even minor ones, produce predictable negative outcomes, while carefully aligned small changes produce massive results. By focusing on small, precise adjustments that reward desired behaviors, leaders can guide predictable behavior toward collective goals efficiently and sustainably. Incentive-aware systems leverage minor changes to produce disproportionate impact across personal, professional, and societal domains. Predictable human behavior ensures that thoughtful, small interventions are among the most effective strategies for transformation. Recognizing and applying the power of small incentives turns everyday decisions into a catalyst for massive, predictable results.

CHAPTER .40

THE FUTURE BELONGS TO THOSE WHO DESIGN BETTER INCENTIVES

Lasting progress depends on our ability to reward what truly matters and align predictable human behavior with long-term goals.

The future of society, business, and personal development hinges on our capacity to design incentives that align human behavior with desired outcomes. Predictable responses to reward structures determine whether systems produce progress, innovation, and ethical action—or dysfunction, exploitation, and stagnation. Leaders, policymakers, educators, and individuals who master incentive design hold the key to shaping sustainable, resilient systems. Misaligned incentives, even with noble intentions, produce predictable failures and unintended consequences. By consciously aligning incentives with long-term goals, societies and organizations can harness predictable human behavior for constructive outcomes. Incentive-aware design transforms abstract ideals into measurable, enduring results.

Corporate and organizational success increasingly depends on the skill of designing effective incentives. Companies that reward innovation, collaboration, ethical behavior, and long-term value creation consistently outperform those focused on short-term gains, competition, or extraction. Employees respond predictably to the reward structures they encounter, meaning alignment between incentives and organizational goals drives sustained performance. Misaligned incentives produce predictable disengagement, risk-taking, or unethical behavior that undermines success. By consciously shaping compensation, recognition, and career progression, leaders ensure predictable alignment between behavior and organizational objectives. Incentive-aware corporate design becomes the defining factor for resilience, innovation, and ethical growth in the modern economy.

Government, policy, and social systems illustrate the transformative power of incentive-aware design. Citizens, bureaucrats, and institutions act predictably in response to the rewards and penalties embedded in legal, social, and economic frameworks. Policies that reward contribution, transparency, and long-term stewardship foster predictable public trust, engagement, and social cohesion. Misaligned incentives, such as prioritizing short-term wins, political gain, or opportunistic behavior, produce predictable dysfunction, corruption, and inequality. Leaders who align incentives with sustainable societal goals harness predictable human behavior to achieve lasting reform and stability. Incentive-aware governance ensures that civic and institutional behavior reinforces progress rather than undermining it. Designing better incentives is therefore central to shaping the future of functional, equitable societies.

Historical examples highlight the role of incentive design in shaping enduring civilizations. Societies, organizations, and movements that embedded reward structures aligned with contribution, ethics, and long-term growth produced predictable innovation, stability, and prosperity. Conversely, systems that rewarded exploitation, favoritism, or extraction experienced predictable decline, corruption, or collapse. Human behavior responds systematically to incentives, making the mastery of reward design essential for lasting progress. Incentive-aware leaders, reformers, and communities understand that predictable alignment between reward and behavior produces systemic transformation. Those who design better incentives shape the future by turning human tendencies into tools for resilience, creativity, and ethical development. The lessons of history confirm that incentive design determines which systems endure and thrive.

Personal and community action also illustrates the predictive power of incentive-aware design. Families, neighborhoods, professional networks, and social groups respond predictably to rewards, recognition, and reinforcement. Misaligned incentives produce disengagement, conflict, or destructive behavior, while aligned incentives foster cooperation, learning, and growth. Individuals who consciously design the incentives around them shape predictable positive outcomes in behavior, culture, and achievement. Incentive-aware personal leadership ensures that daily actions, habits, and interactions reinforce contribution, ethical behavior, and long-term goals. Predictable human responses make deliberate reward design a high-impact tool for shaping both micro and macro outcomes. The future belongs to those who intentionally create systems where the right behaviors are the most rewarding.

Financial, educational, and technological systems demonstrate the predictive power of incentive-aware design at scale. Investors, students, employees, and users act predictably when reward structures are clear, aligned, and meaningful. Misaligned incentives in these systems produce predictable inefficiency, exploitation, or disengagement. Conversely, systems that reward mastery, contribution, innovation, and long-term growth produce sustainable and predictable outcomes. Leaders who design incentives strategically transform markets, learning platforms, and digital tools into engines of constructive human behavior. Incentive-aware design amplifies the impact of predictable behavior, turning alignment into measurable progress. The future is therefore shaped by those who can harness incentives to guide behavior toward enduring value creation, ethical action, and systemic resilience.

Technology and innovation offer some of the clearest examples of future-defining incentive design. Platforms, tools, and algorithms shape behavior predictably based on the reward structures they embed. Misaligned incentives can produce destructive engagement, misinformation, or exploitation at massive scale. Conversely, systems designed to reward contribution, collaboration, and ethical action produce predictable benefits for users, organizations, and society. Incentive-aware innovation ensures that technology amplifies positive human behavior rather than negative impulses. Leaders and designers who master incentive alignment predictably guide systems toward long-term value, ethical development, and societal benefit. The future belongs to those who design tools and systems that align predictable human behavior with enduring goals.

Finally, mastering the future requires understanding the universal principle of predictable human behavior in response to incentives. Individuals, organizations, and societies act reliably when reward structures are clear, aligned, and meaningful. Misaligned incentives produce predictable dysfunction, while aligned incentives foster cooperation, innovation, and ethical behavior. By consciously designing systems, policies, and personal strategies that reward contribution, mastery, and long-term thinking, predictable outcomes emerge that reinforce progress. Incentive-aware design transforms aspirations into reality, ensuring that human behavior consistently supports desired goals. The future belongs to those who understand that predictable human behavior, guided by better incentives, is the ultimate tool for creating enduring, sustainable, and thriving systems.

Epilogue

The world belongs to those who understand the power of what drives behavior. Systems, organizations, and communities are never neutral—they reward some actions and discourage others, shaping predictable outcomes over time. Mastering incentives is not about manipulation; it is about alignment—ensuring that human behavior naturally supports outcomes that are ethical, sustainable, and constructive.

Every choice you make, every policy you implement, and every reward you offer is a chance to shape behavior intentionally. The chapters in this book are a guide, but the real work begins now: noticing the invisible forces around you and becoming an architect of the outcomes you want to see. When we align human nature with human potential, the future becomes something we can build with intention, integrity, and creativity.

About the Author

Laura Lee is a writer, entrepreneur, and creative strategist who blends insight, innovation, and empathy in her work. Raised in a small town where stories were the bridge between people, she discovered early the power of understanding human behavior and the art of meaningful connection.

As the founder of a successful digital design agency, Laura has helped brands, organizations, and individuals craft identities and systems that reflect clarity, purpose, and heart. Her writing and consulting explore the same principles: intentional action, ethical design, and creating systems that reward contribution over extraction.

Laura believes that influence is never neutral—every choice creates a ripple, and every system shapes behavior. Through her books, creative projects, and consulting, she empowers others to notice the invisible forces that guide life and to design incentives that produce predictable, positive outcomes. This book continues that mission, offering readers a framework to align human behavior with values, purpose, and long-term success.

www.ingramcontent.com/pod-product-compliance
Lightning Source LLC
LaVergne TN
LVHW022035200926
848481LV00003B/694